Understanding
DIVERSITY

Understanding
DIVERSITY

An Introduction to Class, Race, Gender, and Sexual Orientation

Fred L. Pincus

LYNNE
RIENNER
PUBLISHERS

BOULDER
LONDON

Published in the United States of America in 2006 by
Lynne Rienner Publishers, Inc.
1800 30th Street, Boulder, Colorado 80301
www.rienner.com

and in the United Kingdom by
Lynne Rienner Publishers, Inc.
3 Henrietta Street, Covent Garden, London WC2E 8LU

Library of Congress Cataloging-in-Publication Data
Pincus, Fred L.
   Understanding diversity : an introduction to class, race, gender, and sexual orientation /
Fred L. Pincus.
      p.   cm.
   Includes bibliographical references and index.
   ISBN 1-58826-426-2 (hardcover : alk. paper) — ISBN 1-58826-402-5 (pbk. : alk. paper)
   1. Pluralism (Social sciences).   2. Pluralism (Social sciences)—United States.
3. Minorities—United States. 4. Prejudices—United States. 5. Discrimination—United
States.   6. United States—Social conditions—21st century.   I. Title.
HM1271.P56 2006
305.800973—dc22

2005029745

British Cataloguing in Publication Data
A Cataloguing in Publication record for this book
is available from the British Library.

Printed and bound in the United States of America

     The paper used in this publication meets the requirements
(∞) of the American National Standard for Permanence of
     Paper for Printed Library Materials Z39.48-1992.

     5   4   3   2   1

Contents

Preface

WHEN I BEGAN TEACHING THE COURSE "DIVERSITY AND PLURALISM:
An Interdisciplinary Perspective" in 2000, I had to select a book to use.
A handful of anthologies were available at the time, but none of them
did quite what I wanted. Since then, I've used two different anthologies
(and a third in a graduate diversity course that I teach), supplementing
them with handouts and reserve readings.

In the summer of 2002 I had lunch with Lynne Rienner at the American Sociological Association meeting in Atlanta. My book *Reverse
Discrimination: Dismantling the Myth* was in production with her company, and we were discussing future projects over sandwiches. She suggested that I write a diversity textbook that could be used instead of one
of the anthologies. I replied that diversity courses needed anthologies,
but that I would be interested in writing a short, inexpensively priced
book that would be used *with* one of the existing anthologies. This is
how *Understanding Diversity* was conceived.

The manuscript was submitted well before Hurricane Katrina hit
New Orleans in August 2005. One of the post-Katrina controversies
involves the issues of class and race that are central to this book. Some
argue about whether the turgid response of the federal government was
because those left in New Orleans were poor or because they were
black. This is the wrong question. Poor whites and people of color are
all victims. Race and class are intimately connected with one another.
The more important question is how poor and working-class people of
all races can work together to demand a more responsive government
and a more equitable economy.

There have been numerous people who have given me important feedback on various drafts of various chapters. The informal Talkfest group—Marina Adler, Howard Ehrlich, Peter Grimes, Susan Pierce, Natalie Sokoloff, and Jason Weller—had several discussions about the first and last chapters. The students in the honors section of Sociology 321, Race and Ethnic Relations—Ludette Agura, Andrew Aladi, Nicole Lazzaro, and An Nguyen-Gia—provided comments during the fall 2004 semester, and Fran Cramblitt, who team teaches with me, also provided helpful comments.

I'd also like to thank the publisher's three anonymous reviewers for their comments and suggestions. One reviewer sent eight single-spaced pages of comments, most of which I enthusiastically incorporated into the second draft. Then, this reviewer sent an additional two pages of comments on the second draft. I hope s/he is happy with the way the book turned out.

I dedicate this book to my wife, Natalie J. Sokoloff, who introduced me to the concept of intersectionality many years ago. She has been an important intellectual sounding board during our daily walks and around the dinner table. It's always wonderful to be able to walk downstairs from my third-floor study to her second-floor study and ask, "Do you have the book by . . . ?" or "Where can I find something on . . . ?" or "What do you think about this?" She would alert me to diversity-related articles in the *New York Times,* and I would pass along criminal justice–related articles from the *Baltimore Sun.* Since she was working on her own book while I was writing this one, we did not spend hours editing each other's prose or checking each other's spelling. We did, however, continue to share the cooking and other household chores.

—Fred L. Pincus

Understanding
DIVERSITY

1

Introduction

MOST OF US GROW UP IN A WORLD THAT SEEMS FAIRLY HOMO-
geneous. Our neighbors and schoolmates are generally from the same
race and social class as we are. Between 5 and 10 percent of the people
in our neighborhoods are probably gay or lesbian, although many of us
don't know who they are.

Upon entering college, students often feel assaulted by diversity,
especially those who live in campus residence halls. Suddenly, room-
mates or those on the same floor can be of different races, religions, ethnicities, and economic backgrounds. Some are from different regions of
the United States and even from different countries. The sounds and
smells and visual images are often unfamiliar. Men and women may
live on the same floor. A gay person may live a few doors down, or in
the same suite. Sexual relations with the opposite sex (or with the same
sex) are not supervised, and alcohol and drugs are everywhere.

Walking around the campus, it is not unusual to see tables and signs
promoting the women's union, the black student union, the gay liberation organization, and international student organizations. You can take
courses such as "Black History," "Women's Literature," and "Gay Cin-
ema."

On the one hand, this campus diversity can be very exciting since
there can be new and stimulating experiences every day. On the other
hand, it can be very disconcerting. Are people who speak Spanish talking about you? Is that gay person down the hall checking you out? Do
you feel embarrassed that someone of the opposite sex sees you in your
nightclothes or without makeup? Why are those guys down the hall so
loud, or so quiet? That music is awful; how can they like it? Are they

1

going to rob me? It's not always easy to be around people who are different from you.

For better or worse, *diversity* has become one of the buzzwords of the early twenty-first century. Two-thirds of colleges and universities have some kind of diversity requirement in their curricula, and many have ethnic and/or women's studies programs. Increasing numbers of large corporations have diversity departments that include recruiters, trainers, and troubleshooters. Politicians, including many conservatives, and the media often extol the history of immigration that has made the United States a pluralistic society characterized as a melting pot, a salad bowl, or a patchwork quilt.

There is another side to the diversity picture, however. Colleges and universities are accused of being too "politically correct" in their "pandering" to minority groups. Corporations are accused of hiring "unqualified" minorities and women in order to satisfy federal affirmative action guidelines. "Reverse discrimination" against white males is said to have replaced traditional discrimination in the eyes of many white Americans.

Many mainstream politicians and media commentators are concerned about how contemporary immigration is allegedly threatening the integrity of American culture and the English language. In my own state of Maryland, for example, in spring 2004, the state comptroller (a Democrat) had difficulty communicating with a recent immigrant who worked at the takeout counter of a local fast-food restaurant. He complained to the press that immigrants don't try hard enough to learn English and that "they" should adjust to "us" rather than the other way around. The next day, the governor (a Republican) publicly agreed with the comptroller and then criticized the "multicultural crap" that was taught in the public schools. This precipitated a huge controversy in the local media that lasted several weeks.

Gay marriages and civil unions became a national controversy in 2004 after the Massachusetts Supreme Court permitted same-sex marriages and several jurisdictions in California, Oregon, and New York began issuing marriage licenses (which were subsequently invalidated) to same-sex couples. In response, conservatives, supported by President George W. Bush, began promoting a constitutional amendment that would limit marriage to one man and one woman.

Labor unions have been redefined as "special-interest" groups, and politicians who talk about growing economic inequality are accused of fomenting class conflict, whereas corporations are thought to represent the interests of the entire country. Women have also been defined as a special-interest group, and pro-choice advocates have been redefined as "baby killers," in contrast to anti-abortionists and those who still believe that women's place is in the home, who are said to be "protectors of family values."

Even the term *liberal* has become controversial. In the 2004 presidential election, the only people using the L-word were conservative Republicans when they criticized Democratic candidate John Kerry as a "tax and spend liberal" who "panders to special interests." Democrats, in comparison, did everything they could to dissociate Kerry from the L-word. There is no doubt that the debate over diversity will continue during the foreseeable future.

Defining Diversity

What is diversity? According to Merriam-Webster Online (2004), **diversity** means *variety, multiformity, difference, or dissimilarity.* The opposite of diversity is uniformity. This can apply to people, cultures, plants, animals, and a number of other topics. From a social science perspective, this definition is not very helpful because it is much too broad.

There are at least four ways that social scientists use the concept of diversity. **Counting diversity** refers to *empirically enumerating differences within a given population.* In a given country (or state, city, school, workplace), we can count how many members of different races, ethnicities, religions, genders, and so on, there are. A particular country can be described as relatively homogeneous if most people are of the same race (religion, ethnicity, etc.) or relatively heterogeneous if there are many different races. Although this may seem uncontroversial, we will see how difficult it is to actually determine who is in what race.

Culture diversity, on the other hand, refers to *the importance of understanding and appreciating the cultural differences between groups.* The focus here is on how rich and poor, whites and people of color, men and women, and homosexuals and heterosexuals have different experiences, worldviews, modes of communication, and behaviors as well as different values and belief systems. Those who use this definition tend to seek lower levels of prejudice, higher levels of tolerance, and more inclusion so that diversity can be celebrated. Usually, the assumption is that appropriate attitudinal changes can take place without large-scale structural changes in the economic and political systems.

Good-for-business diversity refers to the argument that *businesses will be more profitable, and government agencies and not-for-profit corporations will be more efficient, with diverse labor forces.* Supporters of this definition would argue, for example, that a female car salesperson would be more effective than a man in selling cars to women customers. Along the same lines, a Hispanic police officer would do a better job than a white in policing the Hispanic community. Not having diverse employees, according to this view, is simply bad for business.

Finally, **conflict diversity** refers to *understanding how different groups exist in a hierarchy of inequality in terms of power, privilege, and wealth*. Scholars who use this definition emphasize the way in which dominant groups oppress subordinate groups who seek liberation, freedom, institutional change, and/or revolution. Calls to celebrate diversity within a fundamentally unjust system, according to this perspective, are insufficient.

Although these definitions are not always mutually exclusive, this book utilizes the conflict diversity definition described above. I will analyze the conflicts based on class, race, gender, and sexual orientation in the United States.

The Study of Diversity

Studying group conflict within the population is nothing new. Sociologists and historians have been studying immigration and race relations for more than a century. W. E. B. DuBois and Robert Park conducted empirical studies in the early twentieth century, and other scholars debated whether the appropriate metaphor for American race and ethnic relations was the "melting pot" or the "salad bowl" or "anglo-conformity." Karl Marx and Max Weber wrote about class inequality in the nineteenth century. Both race relations and social stratification have for decades been recognized as legitimate sociological specializations. Although a few scholars had been studying male-female conflicts in the early twentieth century, the social scientific study of gender inequality exploded in the 1960s, soon to be followed by a dramatic growth in the study of homosexuality.

Black/African-American studies programs began to develop in the late 1960s, with Hispanic, Asian, and Native American studies emerging in the next few decades. Women's studies programs were first institutionalized in the 1970s, followed by gay and lesbian studies. The field of working-class studies is still in its infancy.

Most of these earlier approaches, however, tended to focus on only one group or category at a time. Race relations, for example, tended to focus on racial differences without considering class and gender. Stratification studies tended to ignore gender and race. Almost all academic programs ignored sexual orientation.

Eventually, increasing numbers of scholars, especially women, grew to understand that it was necessary to go beyond single categories. Predominantly white socialist feminists began to use both class and gender in their analyses, and black feminists began to incorporate race and class. Multiculturalists, especially in the field of education, crossed the boundaries of race, religion, ethnicity, and nationality.

It wasn't until the late 1980s that social scientists began to systematically discuss race, class, gender, and sexual orientation *together*. The first edition of Paula Rothenberg's *Race, Class, and Gender in the United States* was published in 1988 under the title *Racism and Sexism: An Integrated Study*. Margaret L. Anderson and Patricia Hill Collins published the first edition of *Race, Class, and Gender* in 1992. The scholarly journal *Race, Gender, and Class* began publication in 1993 under the editorship of Jean Belkhir. Bonnie Thornton Dill and Maxine Baca Zinn's *Women of Color in US Society* was published in 1994. Even in specialty areas like criminal justice, Barbara Price and Natalie Sokoloff used a race-class-gender approach in the first edition of their anthology *The Criminal Justice System and Women*.

I had been teaching race and ethnic relations for twenty-seven years when I first got interested in the broader topic of diversity in 1996. I was never satisfied with the way I handled class and gender in my own teaching, and I totally ignored sexual orientation. I also began to realize that most undergraduates left the university without any exposure to women's studies, black studies, or any other aspect of diversity. In 1999 I took over teaching a graduate course called "Constructing Race, Class, and Gender" when the person who designed the course left the university. I include sexual orientation even though it isn't in the title.

For several years, I worked with an interdisciplinary committee to design an introductory undergraduate course that came to be called "Diversity and Pluralism: An Interdisciplinary Perspective." The course is team-taught by a pair of faculty who are "demographically different" from one another and are also from different departments. This book grew out of the "Diversity and Pluralism" course.

▓ Levels of Analysis

Understanding conflict diversity is incredibly complex. After teaching about these issues for more than thirty-five years, I have come to realize that there are no simple causes of, or solutions to, group conflict. In 1992 after a jury acquitted the white police officers that were shown on videotape beating Rodney King, a black man, a four-day riot took place in Los Angeles, resulting in 52 deaths, 8,000 injuries, 12,000 arrests, and $800 million in property damage. During the melee, a distraught Rodney King asked, "Why can't we just get along?" A simple question, but a complex answer.

Like most social phenomena, it is necessary to look at group conflict from different levels of analysis. In the United States, we are used to *individualizing* group conflict and other social problems. Why did some individuals riot while others did not? Are there personality differences, or attitudinal differences, or differences in the family structures of their homes? How can they be caught and punished so that it won't happen again? Although these are certainly legitimate questions, they don't tell the whole picture.

It is also necessary to look at group conflict from the *structural* level by looking at the society in which the conflict took place. How does wealth, income, and unemployment differ between those who were rioting and those whose property was damaged? Why were most of the rioters male rather than female? What kind of political power did the rioters have in the city? What role did the economy play? How does the police department treat blacks and Hispanics relative to whites and Asians? What kinds of cultural images of different groups are portrayed in the schools and in the media? Why do most Americans see the riot as blacks versus whites and Asians, when the majority of those arrested were Hispanic? These questions address the nature of the entire society, not just the individuals that are involved in a particular event.

In order to understand both the individual and structural levels of analysis, we must look at group conflict in an interdisciplinary way. We can't be limited by any one discipline. For example, how can we explain the fact that among year-round full-time workers, women earn only $0.79 for each $1.00 that a man earns? At the psychological level, we may try to understand why an individual woman decides to enter a predominantly female profession such as teaching, which pays less than a predominantly male profession such as engineering. At the historical level, we can learn how and why teaching and clerical work changed from being predominantly male occupations to predominantly female ones. At the economic level, we can learn why clerical workers earn less than truck drivers even though they have comparable levels of skill. At the sociological level, we can learn how family structures and gender role socialization have a strong influence on the world of work. Using the tools of only one academic discipline will always be incomplete.

The need for an interdisciplinary and multilevel analysis puts a great burden on those of us who teach and write about diversity from a group conflict perspective. Most of us have been trained to look at social phenomena from only one discipline, so we must educate ourselves about intellectual approaches that we didn't learn in graduate school. It is often difficult to find faculty to teach diversity courses because of the intellectual challenges that these courses pose.

It also puts a great burden on students who are trying to understand the world in which they live. Many students enroll with the hope that they will find an answer to Rodney King's question, "Why can't we just get along?" What they find is that the answer is much more complicated than they ever imagined.

■ The Rest of the Book

This book is intended to be a companion to one of the anthologies that address race, class, gender, and sexual orientation. The strength of anthologies is their breadth in providing descriptions and analyses of many different groups. They have articles on prejudice toward several different racial groups, not just blacks. There may be one article about discrimination against working-class white women and another about discrimination against middle-class Asian women. An article about the health problems of gay men could be contrasted with another about the process of going through a sex-change operation.

However, these same anthologies often do not provide a careful discussion of basic concepts or systematic comparisons between groups or up-to-date statistical data. This is what I will try to do in this short book. Some of the anthologies also include discussions about age, disability, and religion, but I will leave that to others.

Chapter 2 will introduce some of the basic analytical concepts that are used in the study of diversity. Students who are also using one of the anthologies will benefit from having these concepts clearly defined in a single chapter. However, since social scientists don't always agree on these important concepts, the definitions in this book may not always be the same as the definitions in your anthology. A listing of all the key terms used in the book can be found at the book's end.

Chapters 3, 4, 5, and 6 will cover the issues of class, race, gender, and sexual orientation, respectively. Each of these chapters will have a similar structure:

1. show how the concepts discussed in Chapter 2 apply and introduce new concepts;
2. present descriptive statistics about differences in wealth, income, unemployment, education, occupation, and so on;
3. discuss the research on prejudice and ideology;
4. discuss the research on discrimination and structure.

Chapter 7 will address the issue of change and will emphasize the importance of collective social action. A list of activist organizations that students can join is provided.

Some of the material we will be dealing with may be unsettling. Students will no doubt agree with some things and strongly disagree with others. I encourage you to plunge in and keep an open mind. I invite you to question and challenge the issues discussed in this book. If you don't understand something, ask your instructor. If you disagree with something, ask your classmates what they think.

I also encourage you to disagree with your instructor and your classmates—in a respectful manner, of course. I hope your instructor has provided a safe and comfortable atmosphere in which to discuss some of these issues. Many of the students in my classes say that this was the first time they were able to discuss race and gender issues with people different from themselves. I invited a lesbian speaker to one class toward the end of a semester to answer questions about sexual orientation; three students came out on that day. Another student told me that he was going to be absent for two weeks because he was going on a *hadj* (Islamic pilgrimage) in Mecca. He conducted a wonderful question-and-answer session with the class when he got back.

I encourage you to read the newspapers and watch television news with a new, critical perspective. When you watch TV sit-coms, you will be able to see the gender stereotyping that goes on. On crime shows, what are the race and class of the criminals compared with the police and the lawyers? How are gay people presented, if at all?

I promise that by the end of the book, you will have a much different understanding of diversity and group conflict than you do now. Perhaps you will begin to look at the world in a different way. That's how change begins.

2

Basic Concepts
of Diversity

WHEN I ENROLLED IN MY FIRST SOCIOLOGY CLASS MORE THAN forty years ago, the instructor said that we would be learning "soc-speak." By that, he meant that we would be learning some of the terminology that sociologists use to communicate with each other. Some of my classmates argued that sociology was nothing but using jargon to describe what everyone already knows. Although this characterization of sociology is overly harsh, it's certainly the case that professional jargon sometimes makes it exceedingly difficult to understand what is being discussed.

All academic disciplines, including the study of diversity, have their own jargons that make it easier to communicate. Some of the concepts are shared by all members of a discipline and have common definitions. Other concepts are quite contentious, and people argue over their definitions. Sometimes there are also arguments about whether the concepts are appropriate to use at all.

In this chapter I'd like to introduce you to some of the important general concepts used in the study of diversity. In my former instructor's tradition, we can call this "diverspeak." I will concentrate on concepts that will appear throughout the book. Some concepts, such as racism and sexism, I will discuss in other chapters because they are both contentious and somewhat narrower in scope. The concepts will appear in **boldface** and the definitions in *italics*.

▓ Master Status

Two of the most basic concepts in sociology are status and role. **Status** refers to *a position that one holds or a category that one occupies in a society.* Each individual holds many positions and belongs to many categories. For example, a particular person can be white, female, mother, sister, child, worker, neighbor, middle age, suburbanite, flute player, and so on. Each of these statuses has a culturally defined **role** that *specifies expected behavior that goes along with a specific status.* Teachers, for example, are supposed to help students learn certain content, treat students fairly, correct papers, issue grades, and so on. Students are supposed to attend class, study hard, and respect the teacher.

In a diverse society like ours, however, people don't always agree on the appropriate behavior that should be associated with a particular status. For example, some would say that "good" mothers are supposed to stay home and take care of children, whereas others would say that good mothers can have jobs outside of the home. More important, within a particular culture, "appropriate" roles might look different at different levels of society. From a boss's perspective, for example, workers trying to organize a union might be viewed as troublemakers and be fired. From a worker's perspective, in contrast, organizing a union might be one of the few ways of trying to improve their lives.

Although we all occupy many different statuses, some are more important than others. In my own life, for example, being a white, male, heterosexual professional had a much greater impact on me than being Jewish, a resident of Baltimore, or a neighbor. A **master status** is *one that has a profound effect on one's life, that dominates or overwhelms the other statuses one occupies* (Rosenblum and Travis 2003, 33). In our society, master statuses include race, class, gender, and sexual orientation. Age and disability can also be viewed as master statuses, but they will not be discussed in any depth in this book. These master statuses have a much stronger impact on our lives than things like being a friend or a chess player.

Master statuses are culturally determined, not a matter of individual choice. I know people, for example, whose religion is the most important part of their self-identity. In our country, however, social scientists don't usually view religion as a master status since it usually does not determine how one is perceived and treated by the larger society. Although members of some religions, such as Islam, have been viewed with some suspicion in the United States, this has not yet risen to the level where religion is a master status. In the Middle East, religion would be considered to be a master status given the political and cultural conflicts in that area.

▓ Dominant and Subordinate Groups

Within each of the four master statuses that we will be discussing, some groups have more power and influence than others. A **dominant group** *is a social group that controls the political, economic, and cultural institutions in a society.* In contrast, a **subordinate group** *is a social group that lacks control of the political, economic, and cultural institutions in a society.*

In the area of race in the United States, for example, whites are the dominant group and people of color are the subordinate groups. Students of race relations have traditionally used the terms *majority group* and *minority group* to describe dominant and subordinate groups, respectively. People of color (nonwhites) in the United States are minority groups both numerically and in terms of power. However, if one were to apply this terminology to South Africa during apartheid, the white numerical minority would be called the majority group because it had power, and the black numerical majority would be called the minority group. Because power is more important than numbers in studying diversity, I will use the terms *dominant* and *subordinate*.

In terms of gender, men are the dominant group and women the subordinate group. In terms of sexual orientation, heterosexuals are the dominant group. The subordinate group, however, is made up of a variety of groups that challenge traditional definitions of sexual orientation, including gays (male homosexuals), lesbians (female homosexuals), bisexuals (those who are sexually attracted to both males and females), and transgendered people (whose identity is inconsistent with their biological makeup). Collectively, this group is often referred to as "GLBT" people.

There are also dominant and subordinate groups in terms of class, although this is not well thought-out in our society. Although this will be discussed more in Chapter 3, I will call the wealthiest 1 or 2 percent of the population the dominant group. The subordinate group consists of the large majority of the population who work for a living or who want to work and can't find decent jobs.

▓ Social Construction

In discussing race and gender, most Americans assume that there is something biological that differentiates whites from other races and men from women. This view, called **essentialism**, means that *reality exists independently of our perception of it; i.e., that there are real and important (essential) differences among categories of people* (Rosenblum and Travis 2003, 33). Essentialists would also argue that there are also biological differences between heterosexuals and GLBT people.

According to essentialists, then, racial groups can scientifically be differentiated by skin color, hair texture, facial shape, or other genetic characteristics. Men and women can be differentiated by primary and secondary sexual characteristics, hormones, body shape, and so on. Finally, essentialists would argue that homosexuals have some differences in areas of the brain or some other genetic characteristic that predisposes them to be attracted to people of the same sex.

The **social constructionist** perspective argues that *reality cannot be separated from the way a culture makes sense of it—that meaning is "constructed" through social, political, legal, scientific, and other processes* (Rosenblum and Travis 2003, 33). This means that in the United States, there are socially and culturally defined reasons that people are assigned to being white, black, Asian, or Native American that may have nothing to do with biological categories. For example, although we say that skin color is the defining characteristic, some people who are culturally defined as "black" have lighter skins than some people who are culturally defined as "white." Should a person with an Asian mother and a black father be defined as either Asian or black, as opposed to being in a separate "mixed race" category? Racial categories are not real in a biological sense, but they are real in a social or cultural sense: people who are defined as white are treated differently from people defined as black. We will discuss this in much more detail in Chapter 4.

Along the same lines, the distinction between male and female can be problematic among people with ambiguous sexual organs or who have both male and female sexual organs. What should we call someone who is genetically female but who has a penis? What should we call someone who was born genetically male but who has a sex-change operation, or someone who is genetically female but dresses and acts like a man? We usually try to fit people into one category or the other, but the decisions are often arbitrary (see Chapter 5).

Sexual orientation is also a problematic category to define. Most people would have no trouble saying that a woman who has sexual relations with other women throughout her life is a homosexual/lesbian. However, what do we call someone who has occasional homosexual relations but is in a long-term heterosexual relationship? How about someone who was in a homosexual relationship for one year of his or her life but was otherwise heterosexual? There are also people who are attracted to people of the same sex but who are celibate. Our culture tries to force people into one or the other category, but this has nothing to do with biology or with other essentialist criteria (see Chapter 6).

The essentialist/constructionist distinction can also be applied to the category of class. Although most people, including social scientists, don't equate class with any biological reality, there is still the widespread belief that terms like "middle class" or "poor" actually refer to something essential or real. Social scientists often quantify the percentage of the population that is in various classes. The United States is often called "a middle-class society."

Constructionists argue that these class divisions are often arbitrary and are quite variable from one social scientist to another. Marxists, for example, argue that the majority of Americans are *working* class, with the poor being included as the lowest level of the working class. Others don't even use the term *working class* and say that there is a "lower middle class" that is separate from the "lower class" or "poor." Some social scientists define the upper class as those in the top 10 percent of the income distribution, but they don't differentiate those who make $200 million per year from those who make $200,000. We will discuss the social construction of class in more detail in Chapter 3.

Sometimes the concept of social construction is easier to see if we look at other countries. In Latin America, for example, class is seen as a more important concept than race even though lighter-skinned people are more economically privileged than darker-skinned people. Race is seen as a more continuous category rather than the "either-or" category that often exists in the United States. I've had many Latin American students who hadn't even thought much about race in their own countries until they took my course.

In Great Britain, a formal aristocracy based on family lineage still exists, though it has much less power than in the past. Eligibility for the House of Lords, one of the two houses of the parliament, is based on family background, though the House of Commons is responsible for most legislation. Although there are "high society" lists in some major cities in the United States, we do not have a formal aristocracy.

The important point to take away from this discussion is that the master statuses and their subcategories are all socially constructed in each society. There is nothing real about them in either an essential or a biological sense.

■ Oppression

Some concepts, such as oppression, are frequently used in an imprecise and rhetorical way without being carefully defined. Often, an oppressed group is thought of as being extremely poor and/or living in a ruthless authoritarian police state filled with random acts of violence. The lack of a clear definition is most unfortunate in the study of diversity since the concept of oppression is central to understanding group conflict. After reviewing definitions put forward by a variety of writers, I have settled on the following definition, adapted from Blauner (1972): **oppression** *is a dynamic process by which one segment of society achieves power and privilege through the control and exploitation of other groups, which are burdened and pushed down into the lower levels of the social order.*

Several important implications follow from this definition. First, since oppression involves power, only the dominant group can be the oppressors, and only the subordinate groups can be the oppressed. In the area of gender, for example, we can say that women are oppressed because they are pushed down by the legal system, the economic system, and/or the family structure. Many writers have observed that one of the difficulties that men face is the inability to express emotions to women and to other men; although this is a limitation that may prevent men from achieving their full potential, it is not an example of oppression because men tend to control most of the dominant social institutions (Frye 1983). Similarly, whites are not oppressed by racism even though their prejudiced attitudes may prevent them from forming friendships with people of color.

The term **exploitation** means that *the dominant group uses the subordinate group for its own ends, including gaining economic profit and maintaining a higher position in the social hierarchy.* In the area of class oppression, for example, employers try to keep wages as low as possible so that their profits can be as high as possible. In the area of racial oppression, whites have used housing and educational segregation as a way of controlling the more desirable neighborhoods and schools. In the traditional male-controlled family, men often have their meals cooked, their houses cleaned, and their children taken care of through the unpaid labor of their spouses.

The oppression and exploitation of homosexuals by heterosexuals are more social and cultural than economic. Since only heterosexual romantic/sexual relations are widely accepted, homosexuals are at the bottom of the social hierarchy and are often shunned, harassed, and physically brutalized.

In a society characterized by oppression, some groups have more privileges than others. **Privilege** means that *some groups have something of value that are denied to others simply because of the groups they belong to; these unearned advantages give some groups a head start in seeking a better life.* Understanding this concept may be difficult, especially for those who are privileged.

In some cases, privileges are quite subtle—at least to those who have them. Heterosexuals, for example, assume that it's okay for them to display a picture of their significant other on their desk at work or to hold hands in a public place. Gays and lesbians, in comparison, are often wary about displaying this type of public affection, often with good reason.

A white customer in a store can usually assume that those who work in the store assume that the customer is there to purchase a product. Black customers, however, are often viewed with suspicion and followed or watched by the store staff since they are not assumed to be legitimate customers.

In both of these "subtle" examples, members of the dominant groups (i.e, heterosexual office workers and white store customers) are simply going about business as usual, as they should. The problem is that they usually don't realize that the very same behavior by members of subordinate groups (homosexual office workers and black customers) is viewed quite differently. Business as usual for subordinate groups is not the same as for dominant groups.

In other cases, privilege is not at all subtle. Upper-income families, for example, usually can afford to live in a safe neighborhood and to send their children to high-quality schools. The children benefit because of the family that they were lucky to be born into. Working-class and poor families have fewer options, and their children will live in less safe neighborhoods and attend lower-quality schools. Similarly, men have a chance to compete for a number of high-status, well-paying jobs where the expectation is that the job will probably go to a male. Women, even if they are qualified, have much less of a chance in this competition.

Everyone should have the same opportunity to live in a safe area, attend a high-quality school, enter a fair competition for a job, hold hands with a loved one, and be assumed to be honest. These should be rights of citizenship. The problem is that the dominant groups have much greater access to these privileges than do the subordinate groups.

One of the most important privileges of the dominant group members is not having to know that you are privileged in the first place. They assume, incorrectly, that everyone else has access to the same privileges that they do. When I was teaching my teenage son to drive, for example, I recall reading an article about black parents who were teaching their sons to drive. One important lesson that the black teenagers learned was to keep their hands on the steering wheel if they were stopped by the police. This, hopefully, would reduce any accidental shootings by the police, who might think a black driver was reaching for a weapon. I never even dreamed of talking to my own white son about this. Members of the subordinate groups can more easily recognize the existence of privilege than members of the dominant group.

When I discuss privilege and oppression in class, I often get two reactions from members of dominant groups. Some of the privileged feel guilt and/or discomfort in learning that they are privileged. They want to cast off their privilege in order to maintain their image of being a fair-minded person. Responding to these feelings, Alan Johnson (2001, 15) argues that privilege and oppression are "rooted in a legacy we all inherited, and while we're here, it belongs to us. It isn't our fault. It wasn't caused by something we did or didn't do. But now that it's ours, it's up to us to decide how we're going to deal with it before we collectively pass it along to the generations that will follow ours."

Other members of the privileged react with denial. A working-class white male student, for example, raises his hand and says, "I'm not privileged; I've had to fight for everything that I got." Often, this comment is followed by an angry but heartfelt story of someone from a poor family who really did have to struggle in life, including having to work and take out loans to pay for college. "And I had to do it without the benefits of affirmative action," he continues. Other white males (and some females) often nod in agreement, suggesting that the concept of race and gender privilege is a figment of my imagination.

My response usually is to say that the student's story is one that reflects *class* oppression, something we don't talk about very much in our society. The student lacks *class* privilege even though he still has race and gender privilege. We in the United States often attribute economic oppression only to race, because class remains largely invisible.

This illustrates the important point that people can be in the oppressor group with regard to one master status but in the oppressed group with regard to another. My student still has some of the privileges of being white, but he lacks the privileges of being wealthy or middle-income. Not all members of the oppressor group benefit in the same way, and not all members of the oppressed group are harmed in the same way. Sometimes this neutralizes the anger somewhat, since students have gained a broader way to understand the complex reality of oppression and privilege.

Using the discourse of oppression is really quite subversive in the United States. We often like to think of ourselves as a classless society that is gradually breaking down barriers of race, sex, and possibly even sexual orientation. Assimilation, inclusion, and upward mobility are the preferred discourse, not oppression, exploitation, and privilege. According to conservatives, opposition to President George W. Bush's 2003 tax cuts that favored the wealthy was said to promote class conflict, whereas the tax cuts themselves were said to be good for all Americans. Women's groups, unions, and gay rights groups were called "special interests," but conservatives who defend big business and male-dominated families were said to be protecting traditional American values.

▥ Culture, Attitudes, and Ideology

Diversity and group conflict also have important attitudinal components in terms of how different groups see one another. This is reflected in the culture as well as in how individuals think, feel, and believe. Privileged groups, being dominant groups in terms of power, usually have the ability to define nonprivileged groups in an "us" versus "them" type of way. When a subordinate group is defined as the **"other,"** it is *viewed as being unlike the dominant group in profoundly different, usually negative, ways.* Groups that are "othered" are often seen as inferior, dangerous, and/or immoral. This is more than simply being seen as different.

This "othering" process is not inevitable when different groups come into contact with one another. Theoretically, the dominant racial group could view other groups as interesting curiosities rather than evil competitors. Men could view women as having different dispositions rather than as a weaker group to be dominated. *Different* does not have to mean inferior or threatening.

Groups defined as the "other" are usually stigmatized in a variety of ways. **Stigma** is an *attribute for which someone is considered bad, unworthy, or deeply discredited because of the category that he or she belongs to.* Being a homosexual is viewed by many as grounds for social ostracism, no matter what else that person might have accomplished. In

Nazi Germany, in fact, homosexuals were required to wear pink triangles to differentiate them from the rest of the population, just as Jews were required to wear yellow stars. In the present era, being on welfare is seen as a stigma.

Othering and stigmatization are both *social* processes that influence how given individuals may think. The same is true for **stereotypes**, which are *cultural beliefs about a particular group that are usually highly exaggerated and distorted, even though they may have a grain of truth.* Stereotypes are passed down from one generation to the next, often through the mass media.

Gay males are supposed to act feminine ("swishy"), and lesbians are thought to look masculine ("butch"). These images are often promoted by comedians, television, and the movies, and though a minority of gays and lesbians fit this stereotype, most homosexuals are indistinguishable from heterosexual men and women.

According to another stereotype, blacks in our society are supposed to be naturally talented at basketball and football. Even though blacks are highly overrepresented in the National Basketball Association and the National Football League (this is the grain of truth), it's safe to say that most blacks, like most whites, have only average ability in these two sports.

These athletic stereotypes were brought home to me when I was coaching my son's peewee league basketball team some years ago. Two black boys were among the dozen children that were assigned to the team, and I was thrilled for two reasons: I was happy the team was integrated, and I hoped that the black boys would raise the level of skill of the team. The first child did not disappoint me; he was a mini Michael Jordan. The second child, whom I'll call James, was a tall, broad-shouldered child who looked like the perfect center. The first time the ball was passed to him, James fumbled it, picked it up and fumbled it again, and finally picked it up a third time, tucked it under his arm, and ran with it like a football player. He had no conception of dribbling, he couldn't jump, and he knew absolutely nothing about basketball. So much for the natural talent stereotype.

In addition to being inaccurate, stereotypes often portray the group in question in negative ways. The black basketball image stereotype is part of a more general stereotype that blacks can only excel physically, not intellectually. It also goes along with the "dumb athlete" stereotype. In addition, the swishy/butch homosexual images are often objects of derision.

In this whole process of othering, stigmatization, and stereotyping, the negative attitudes are part of a social process whereby the dominant group oppresses the subordinate group. The negative attitudes, in this view, act as justification for the political and economic oppression. In other words, the oppression causes the negative attitudes, not the other way around. The implication here is that it would be impossible to get rid of the negative attitudes until the oppression is eliminated.

Traditional social psychologists, however, often don't use this approach. Instead, they focus on the concept of **prejudice**, which generally refers to *negative attitudes toward a specific group of people*. This refers to what people think, feel, and believe. Although most of the research on prejudice has taken place in the context of studying race and ethnic relations, the concept can also be applied to gender, sexual orientation, and class. Although some prejudice clearly incorporates cultural stereotypes, there are a variety of other interpersonal dynamics that may be involved as causal factors.

The nature of prejudice can change over time, both in content and intensity. Some social scientists, for example, have argued that antiblack prejudice on the part of whites has dropped dramatically in the years since the 1950s. They present evidence that white Americans are less supportive of segregation, are less likely to stereotype blacks, and are less likely to accept biological explanations of black inferiority. Others counter that although this traditional prejudice has declined, it has been replaced by a new form of prejudice that is still quite intense. We will return to this argument in Chapter 4.

Although othering, stigmatization, and stereotyping tend to come from the dominant group against the subordinate group, prejudice can also be multidirectional. For example, Hispanics' antiwhite attitudes or women's antimale attitudes are just as prejudiced as the anti-Hispanic attitudes held by whites or the antifemale attitudes held by males. Whether one is worse than another, according to this argument, is an empirical question, not a conceptual one; that is, we can compare male attitudes toward females with female attitudes toward males and learn which is more prejudiced. As we will see in subsequent chapters, dominant group prejudice toward subordinate groups tends to be much stronger than any prejudice that exists in the other direction.

The negative attitudes about a particular group can also exist as part of an **ideology**, which is *a body of ideas reflecting the social needs and aspirations of an individual group, class, or culture.* There are several different bodies of ideas, for example, to explain why some people are successful in our society while others are not. One view is that successful people worked hard to get to where they are. According to this view, individual effort can overcome barriers caused by adverse family circumstances or race/gender discrimination. A corollary of this view is the belief that most of those who are not successful didn't work hard enough.

A very different explanation of success, which we might call the "oppressive society" perspective, is that those born into privileged positions are the most likely to be successful because they control the dominant social institutions. A corollary of this view is that less privileged people are usually held back by an unjust society, no matter how hard they work.

Along the same lines, there are different views of the type of equality that should be guaranteed to each citizen. According to the equal opportunity perspective, all citizens should have the same right to compete in the marketplace by selling their labor, investing their money, getting an education, and so on. Presumably, policies that prevent individuals from competing because of their race or gender would be inconsistent with this equal opportunity perspective. However, there is no guarantee of equal results. Suppose a corporation hired ten wealthy white males because they were viewed as the best candidates—that is, they beat out everyone else in a fair and competitive race. This would still be consistent with the equal opportunity perspective. According to this view, the United States is (or should be) a **meritocracy** where *the most skilled people have the better jobs and the least skilled people have the lowest-paying jobs, regardless of race, gender, age, and other factors.*

An alternative perspective on equality could be called the "group rights" perspective. According to this view, dominant groups have unfair advantages in what might appear to be a fair race. For example, although subordinate group members have an abstract right to invest their money, most don't even have enough to live on, much less invest. A few subordinate group individuals might be successful, but most will be left behind. The solution is for the subordinate group to collectively demand that the structure of the race be changed and/or that its members be given the chance to compensate for their lack of privilege.

Ideologies tend to reflect the interests of certain groups in society. The "hard work" and "equal opportunity" perspectives tend to support the positions of the dominant groups because they justify their dominance. In contrast, the "oppressive society" and "group rights" perspectives tend to be critical of the dominant groups and supportive of the right of subordinate groups to fight against oppression as groups, not just as individuals. The goal would be to substantially reduce or eliminate the social and economic differences between different groups.

Within any given culture, *some ideologies are so influential that they dominate all other ideologies.* These dominant perspectives are called

hegemonic ideologies and are widely held by members of both dominant and subordinate groups. Hegemonic ideologies are often invoked by those in power who are trying to enact social policies. In our society, the "hard work" and "equal opportunity" perspectives are the hegemonᵢ views of success and equality. Describing the United States as an oᵣ sive society or invoking the idea of "group rights" is often vieᵥ American by politicians and business leaders. As you maᵥ guessed, this book is an attempt to counter hegemoniᵣ

▒ Discrimination

Whereas prejudice refers to what people oᵥ   group think, feel, and believe about members of other groups, **discrimination** *refers to actions that deny equal treatment to persons perceived to be members of some social category or group.* To simplify things, prejudice is what people think, and discrimination is what people do. The following are all examples of discrimination: not renting an apartment to a welfare recipient who can pay the rent, not hiring a homosexual who has the necessary qualifications, not permitting a woman to join a social club when a comparable man would be admitted, and not admitting a well-qualified Native American to a school.

Although the concept of discrimination seems straightforward, it is actually very complex. There are different levels of discrimination; an individual landlord refusing to rent to a Hispanic is not the same as a bank that refuses to grant mortgages to houses in Hispanic communities. The direction of the discrimination is also important. Is the dominant group discriminating against the subordinate group, or is it the other way around? Finally, there is the question of motivation or intentionality; if a particular policy is gender-blind in intent but negatively impacts women more than men, is this discrimination?

I will discuss three different types of discrimination. **Individual discrimination** *refers to the behavior of individual members of one group/category that is intended to have a differential and/or harmful effect on members of another group/category.* Examples of this type of discrimination include attacking a gay person, not allowing a poor person in the corner store, refusing to rent your basement apartment to a black, and not hiring a qualified woman to supervise male workers. These are all actions taken by individuals on their own that are intended to have a differential and/or harmful effect on members of subordinate groups.

Individual discrimination can be multidirectional. Subordinate groups can also practice individual discrimination against dominant groups or against other subordinate groups if they have the resources to do so. A Native American can attack a white person or a black person. A gay landlord can refuse to rent an apartment to heterosexuals. A female employer can refuse to hire a male worker. A poor person, however, couldn't prevent a rich person from entering his or her store because the poor person wouldn't own a store. This is an example of not having the resources to practice a particular type of discrimination. However, the poor person could yell at a rich person or attack that person. All of these examples are actions by one individual in one group against one individual in another group.

Much discrimination, however, involves more than just individuals. **Institutional discrimination** *refers to the policies of dominant group institutions, and the behavior of individuals who implement these policies and control these institutions, that are intended to have a differential and/or harmful effect on subordinate groups.* Laws that separated blacks and whites in the South from the late 1870s through the 1950s are an excellent example of institutional discrimination. Multinational corporations that favor men over women for management jobs are also practicing institutional discrimination. The military's "don't ask, don't tell" policy that prevents homosexuals from being publicly "out" is another example. In all these cases, the policies are practiced by large, dominant group institutions and are intended to have a differential and/or harmful impact on subordinate groups. In most cases, institutional discrimination is the dominant group acting against the subordinate group. Usually, the subordinate group doesn't have the power or resources to practice institutional discrimination against the dominant group, although it is still theoretically possible.

What about institutional discrimination based on class? Clearly, the wealthy act in a variety of ways that are intended to have a differential and/or harmful impact on working people and the poor. Employers try to keep wages low to increase profits. They will abandon one city or even the entire country for another with a cheaper labor force. They don't want to be burdened by health and safety laws that protect workers. Wal-Mart and many other corporations try to prevent workers from unionizing.

There's no question that these things happen all the time, but there is a question about whether the label "institutional discrimination" is appropriate to describe these actions. The basis of the capitalist economic system is for employers to do everything they can to increase their profits, including keeping their labor and production costs as low as possible. Workers often bear the brunt of these policies because they have less power than the employers. However, to describe these practices as "institutional discrimination" would suggest that the capitalist system itself favors employers over employees—another subversive idea. We will return to this issue in Chapter 3.

The third type of discrimination, **structural discrimination,** *refers to policies of dominant group institutions, and the behavior of the individuals who implement these policies and control these institutions, that are race/class/gender/sexuality-neutral in intent but that have a differential and/or harmful effect on subordinate groups.* The policy *impact* is more important than the intent in this kind of discrimination.

Bank mortgage policies, based on family income and assets, tend to disadvantage non-Asian people of color because of their lower incomes. Tests of physical strength that are based solely on upper body strength disadvantage women, who excel more in lower-body strength exercises. Providing fringe benefits only to married partners would disadvantage gay couples who can't get married. Providing federal income tax cuts only to those with incomes disadvantage poor people who have such low incomes that they don't pay any income taxes, although they still pay more regressive sales taxes. All of these policies don't intend to disadvantage subordinate groups, but they do.

The role of structural discrimination can be seen in the transformation of the job of baggage screeners at US airports since September 11, 2001 (Alonso-Zaldivar and Oldham 2002). Prior to the September 11 terrorist attacks in New York and Washington, the majority of those who screened baggage were minority, many of whom were not US citizens. Their average salary was only $11,000 per year, and they were employed by private companies.

Since September 11, Congress passed legislation raising the salary to $23,000–$35,000 per year and requiring baggage screeners to be federal employees. They also must be US citizens, have a ninth-grade reading capacity, and must pass a battery of employment tests. Consequently, the racial composition of baggage handlers has changed dramatically. In September 2002 the majority of baggage handlers were white. This dramatic turnabout was caused by the new requirements that Congress deemed necessary to be an effective baggage handler, yet they had a negative impact on people of color. One can't help wonder what Congress was thinking by making citizenship a requirement of baggage handlers while 31,000 noncitizens have been issued guns and are on active duty in the armed forces.

Some diversity scholars, along with public opinion, restrict the concept of discrimination to intentional actions and policies—individual and institutional. I believe that it is also useful to characterize unintentional actions and policies as structural discrimination to highlight their negative impact. Good people implementing bad policies can be just as harmful as those who intentionally discriminate.

Many diversity scholars put unintentional discrimination in the "institutional discrimination" category along with intentional discrimination. I prefer to keep institutional and structural discrimination conceptually separate since this emphasizes the negative impact of unintentional discrimination. Perhaps capitalism itself is an example of structural discrimination.

It is common for scholars to speak of individual and institutional racism, sexism, and heterosexism rather than discrimination. Other scholars use racism, sexism, and heterosexism to describe prejudiced attitudes rather than discriminatory behavior. Still other scholars use these same terms to refer to a combination of prejudice and discrimination. The lack of consensus about these important concepts can cause a great deal of confusion and misunderstanding. As we proceed through the book, I will try to carefully define these terms in their relevant chapters.

■ Politics and Political Labels

It is impossible to discuss the issue of diversity without also discussing politics. Most Americans restrict the concept of politics to elections and what goes on in government. The only way people can participate in politics, according to this view, is to vote and to write letters to members of the legislature. Although electoral politics is certainly important, this definition is too restrictive. I prefer to define **politics** as *any collective action that is intended to support, influence, or change social policy or social structures.*

With this broader definition, we can think of a whole range of activities that are political. Fighting for a women's or gay studies program on college campuses is political. International protests against the World Trade Organization (WTO) and the International Monetary Fund (IMF) are political. Residents' trying to prevent Wal-Mart from opening a store in their community is political. Organizing a new trade union is political. Boycotting a business that doesn't hire enough people of color is political. Armed struggle, including terrorism, is also political, although it is often immoral and counterproductive.

Of course, the goals of political actions can be quite different. Anti-abortion (sometimes called pro-life) demonstrations have different goals than pro-choice demonstrations. Pro–affirmative action and anti–affirmative action demonstrations also have different goals. Sometimes, there are even political differences within movements like those that oppose the WTO and IMF.

This brings us to the often-used but not-well-defined labels of conservative, liberal, and radical. Most readers have heard these terms many times but are not sure what they mean. This is complicated by the lack of consensus in our society over these labels. In the following paragraphs, I will not provide crisp definitions as I have done throughout this chapter. Instead, I will try to outline some of the themes that people who use these labels share and try to avoid caricaturing those perspectives with which I disagree.

Conservatives

People who call themselves *conservative* are pro-capitalist and believe that the market economy, free of regulation, will result in the greatest good for the greatest number of people. Economic conservatives also believe in a limited federal government so that businesses can make more profits and create jobs, thereby strengthening the economy. Therefore, conservatives generally oppose strong federal regulations (e.g., civil rights, the environment, health, and safety) and favor low taxes. They generally oppose more federal spending for schools, job training, housing, and the like. They tend to subscribe to the "hard work" and "equal opportunity" ideologies mentioned earlier and argue that most poor people are poor because of weak families and a lack of motivation, in part caused by an overly generous welfare system.

Social conservatives, while agreeing with much of the above, spend most of their energy promoting and protecting what they see as traditional family values. They favor male-dominated nuclear families and are strongly opposed to abortion and gay rights. They are also concerned with bringing prayer and creationism back into schools, and they object to the concept of a separation between church and state. Many social conservatives identify themselves as evangelical Christian fundamentalists who believe in a literal interpretation of the New Testament.

Economic and social conservatives don't always agree on important issues. Some economic conservatives, such as California governor Arnold Schwarzenegger and former New York mayor Rudy Giuliani, argue that abortion and gay rights are private matters that the federal government should not be involved with, just as it shouldn't be involved in the economy.

President George W. Bush combines some aspects of each strand of conservatism. Consistent with economic conservatives, he has argued for reducing the role of the federal government and has slashed taxes on corporations and the wealthy, arguing that this will create more jobs. This is the Bush version of trickle-down economics. Even so, he deviated from economic conservatives by creating huge budget deficits and by ordering local schools to participate in an expensive testing program through the No Child Left Behind Act. Most economic conservatives would prefer that the federal government *reduce* its role in education. Bush is also a born-again Christian whose attitudes reflect the social conservative views of opposition to abortion and gay marriage.

Liberals

Liberals are also strongly pro-capitalist, but they have less faith in an unregulated market economy. They believe that an unrestrained free market can generate serious problems (e.g., recession, inflation, environmental problems, the mutual fund scandal, etc.) and that the federal government must provide adequate regulations so that capitalism doesn't self-destruct. They also argue that the federal government has an important role to play in the field of job training and education. Liberals tend to be more tolerant than conservatives when it comes to issues of civil rights, women's rights, gay rights, unions, programs for the poor, and so on. They tend to argue that poverty is caused by a lack of opportunity. The goal of liberals is to have a fairer, more efficient form of capitalism.

I can't emphasize strongly enough that liberals are *not* socialists because they are in favor of a privately owned economy, which is the essence of capitalism. Liberals simply want the government to be more involved in regulation and in helping those who are poor and unemployed through no fault of their own. Most European countries, including those in Scandinavia, are capitalist in that more than 90 percent of the economy is privately owned. They simply have a more generous welfare state than we have here.

Like conservatives, there is a range of views among liberals. Mainstream liberals, sometimes called progressives (e.g., Senator Edward Kennedy and Representative Dennis Kucinich), tend to argue for somewhat more regulation and government spending to help the poor. In contrast, more centrist or "Third Way" liberals, such as former president Bill Clinton and presidential candidate John Kerry, tend to fall somewhere in between mainstream liberals and economic conservatives. It was Clinton, for example, who signed the welfare reform act in 1996 that restricted recipients to only five years of welfare payments over the course of their lifetimes.

Radicals

Most discussions of political labels are restricted to discussing liberals and conservatives. The Pew Research Center for the People and the Press, for example, has an interesting website wherein you can answer a series of questions and be placed in one of nine different political categories (http://typology.people-press.org). However, there is no category to the left of liberal.

Unlike conservatives and liberals, radicals are anti-capitalist in that they see competition, private ownership of the means of production, and profit seeking as major causes of economic inequality and social intolerance. Some are socialists and want to see government ownership of the economy, economic and social planning, and genuine democratic civil institutions. Unfortunately, there are no current models of advanced industrialized societies that they can point to. Other radicals want more of a "mixed economy" that would combine government ownership with a market economy and a more generous welfare state that would include some form of national healthcare, low-cost childcare, more extensive maternity/paternity leave, and so on. Anarchists, in comparison, reject large bureaucratic structures and want small, localized, collectively run institutions. Radicals would hold the "oppressive society" and "group rights" ideologies described earlier and believe that capitalism must be replaced with a more equitable form of economic organization.

*   *   *

In describing these political tendencies, some writers use the terms *left* and *right,* although the meanings of these terms are so variable that the labels are not very useful. The term *right* generally refers to conservatives. The *left* can refer either to liberals or radicals. When conservatives use the term, "left" refers to Bill Clinton, and "extreme left" refers to Edward Kennedy; radicals are often seen as off the political map. When radicals use the term, they call themselves "the left" and refer to Bill Clinton as a "neoliberal" or "conservative liberal." I will try to avoid using the left-right terminology throughout this book. Hopefully, this brief discussion of political tendencies has caused more enlightenment than confusion.

Congratulations. You have made it through this introduction to diverspeak. Because I covered twenty-five concepts in nineteen pages, you have probably found this chapter a little dry. In the rest of the book, I will be using these and other concepts to discuss race, class, gender, and sexual orientation. For your convenience, I have included all the concepts in a list at the back of the book so that you can consult them when necessary. Let us begin.

3

Class

IN MOST DIVERSITY ANTHOLOGIES, THE SECTION ON CLASS COMES after the chapters on race and gender. I decided to discuss class *before* discussing the other issues because most Americans aren't used to thinking in class terms. As I will demonstrate, class provides the context in which conflict over race, gender, and sexual orientation exists.

When discussing economic inequality with my students, I find that they are more comfortable with discussing racial and gender differences than with discussing class differences. Although both race and gender are intimately connected with class, I shall not emphasize these connections in this chapter. By focusing more narrowly on class, my goal is to help students think in class terms, perhaps for the first time.

■ Terminology

Unfortunately, due to the lack of consensus among social scientists about the nature of class, it is impossible to provide a definition with which everyone will agree. Gilbert (1998, 15), for example, defines **class** this way: *"If a large group of families is approximately equal in rank to each other and clearly differentiated from other families, we call these families a social class."* Although this definition has some value, disagreements over the meaning of "rank" and "clearly differentiated" make this and other definitions of limited use.

Mainstream social scientists tend to see class as a rank in the economic **stratification** system. According to Gilbert (1998, 15), *"a stratified society is one marked by inequality, by differences among people* *that are regarded as being higher or lower."* In practice, many social scientists view stratification as a continuous distribution based on income, occupation, or education.

In thinking about class, two economic indicators are used. **Income** *is the amount of money that a family earns from wages and salaries, interest, dividends, rent, gifts, transfer payments (e.g., unemployment insurance and welfare payments), and capital gains (profits from the sale of assets).* Generally, income refers to the money that a family has coming in during a certain period of time.

Wealth, in contrast, *refers to the assets that people own.* In addition to assets like a house, car, and other personal property, wealth includes stocks, bonds, mutual funds, trust funds, business equity, and real estate. Usually, wealth is expressed as *net worth,* which is the value of what you own less the value of what you owe.

Using the income criteria, one can imagine a vertical line whereby families with the lowest incomes are at the bottom and those with the highest incomes are at the top. The US Bureau of the Census routinely divides this income distribution into five quintiles (or fifths), each of which has the same number of families. Social scientists can then attach labels to these quintiles so that the lowest might be called the "lower class" or "poor." The highest might be called the "upper-middle class," and the middle three would be "the middle class." Both these divisions and the labels are arbitrary.

The problem is that social scientists don't agree on how many classes there are or what they should be called. In the above example, there are three different classes. However, there could just as easily have been five—e.g., lower class, working class, lower-middle class, upper-middle class, and upper class. Or the distribution could have been separated into ten deciles (or tenths), each of which could have been given a label. In each case, there is no hard-and-fast distinction between one class and another, except that some have higher incomes than others. Usually the main distinction is between the poor and everyone else, who is referred to as middle-class.

Using this continuous distribution approach minimizes the effect of those with very high incomes. For example, in 2003, the top 5 percent of households had incomes of $156,120 and higher. If we call this the upper-middle class, it means that a family making $156,120 is in the same class as the family of the chief executive officer of a large corporation who makes millions. I will discuss this further in the next section.

Sometimes the occupational category is the key measure of social class, with professionals and managers being the upper-middle class and unskilled blue-collar and service workers being the lower class. Education can also be used as a measure of class, where people with advanced degrees make up the upper-middle class and high school dropouts make up the lower class.

A variation of this theme is to create a measure of socioeconomic status (SES) by combining measures of income, occupation, and education. The simplest way to proceed is to take each of these three variables and dichotomize them, that is, split them into two. For income, those who earn more than the median income would get a score of 1, and those who earn less would get a 0. For occupation, white-collar workers would get a 1 and manual workers would get a 0. For education, those who have more than a high school education would get a 1, and those with a high school education or less would get a 0.

Using this method, everyone who is in the labor force will get a score from 0 to 3. For example, a college-educated corporate executive who earns more than the median income would get a score of 3. A high-school dropout who works as a janitor and earns less than the median income would get a score of 0. Since we have four levels of SES, we can then attach labels to each level. The corporate executive at level 3 might be called "upper-middle class" while the janitor at level 0 might be called "lower class." Although this is more sophisticated than using income alone, we are still left with a continuous distribution of SES scores with arbitrary labels attached to them.

Occasionally, analysts will use a continuous distribution approach with wealth as the main criterion. For example, Dinesh D'Souza (1999), the well-known conservative writer, has developed a six-class model that is based on a combination of wealth and income—super-rich, rich, upper-middle, middle, lower-middle, and poor. Readers may note that in D'Souza's scheme, there is no working class; he has defined it out of existence.

A dramatically different approach to class is provided by neo-Marxists, who use the concepts of wealth and power to differentiate between classes. Economist Michael Zweig (2000), for example, argues that a small group of people (1 or 2 percent of the adult population) own the means of production and have a lot of decision-making power in society. They are called the employer class, or the capitalist class. The majority of the population (62 percent) own very little and have scant decision-making power. This heterogeneous working class includes both blue-collar and white-collar workers and various levels of skill. The poor, according to Zweig, are considered to be the lowest level of the working class. The remaining 36 percent of the population is the middle class, which includes small business owners, freelance artists and writers, upper-level managers who are not wealthy, and highly paid athletes and entertainers.

In this neo-Marxist view, the capitalist class and the working class are in political and economic conflict with each other, with the middle class caught in between them. Since the capitalist class makes its profits from the labor of the working class, the capitalists are always trying to push labor costs lower while the workers are trying to gain more power to increase their incomes and control over the work process. Class is not just a descriptive category, as it is in the stratification perspective, but has important political ramifications.

Although other neo-Marxists agree with the concept of class conflict between the working class and capitalist class, they don't always agree on the number of classes that exist. Erik Olin Wright (1997), for example, has a twelve-class model.

Dennis Gilbert (1998), who is not a Marxist, agrees that there is a small capitalist class at the top of the class structure, but he divides the rest of the population into five additional classes—upper-middle, middle, working, working poor, and lower. For Gilbert, the *source of income* is the key to who is in what class, and the main division is between the top two classes (capitalist and upper-middle) and the other four classes.

Given these divergent and sometimes imprecise views, can we say class is a socially constructed concept? Is the social definition of class more important than its material essence? On the one hand, there certainly are different cultural definitions of class in terms of how many classes there are and what labels should be used. On the other hand, there appears to be something real about class since we can measure income, wealth, and other important variables and we can see that some members of a population have a lot more of these things than other members. It's also clear that people at the upper class levels have more power than those at the lower class levels. The disagreements are about how class works and how it should be measured, not about whether it exists. There appears to be some essence of class even though there is no unity about what it is.

Another important concept is **social mobility**, which refers to *individuals moving up or down in terms of their class level.* The belief in upward mobility is an important part of American mythology, which is encapsulated into the "log cabin to White House" journey of Abraham Lincoln. We will examine the extent of upward mobility in the next section. Sociologists talk about two types of mobility. **Intergenerational mobility** *refers to a child's class position relative to the child's parents.*

Former president Bill Clinton came from a modest background and was upwardly mobile relative to his parents. President George W. Bush, in contrast, was born into a wealthy and powerful family, so he was not socially mobile. **Intragenerational mobility** *refers to the degree to which a young worker who enters the labor force can improve his or her class position within a single lifetime.* This is the "stock clerk to CEO" version of upward mobility.

Some diversity writers characterize the economic inequality associated with capitalism as a form of **classism**, that is, *a system that stigmatizes poor and working-class people and their cultures and assigns high status to the affluent and their culture solely because of their relative wealth* (Cyrus 2000, 6). Other writers define classism as *prejudice and discrimination based on socioeconomic level or class* (Blumenfeld and Raymond 2000, 25). In this view, class oppression is equivalent to racism, sexism, and heterosexism in terms of importance.

■ Descriptive Statistics

Since there is no consensus on the definition of class, it is difficult to say who is in what class and how many people are in what class. However, it is not at all difficult to describe the degree of economic inequality that exists in the United States. The federal government collects a great deal of economic data, and I will use some of it here.

The distribution of income in 2003 is presented in Table 3.1. On the top half of the table, all households are separated into quintiles, or five categories with the same number of households in each. Twenty percent, or one-fifth, of households earn between $0 and $17,984 annually. If we look at the combined income of these 22 million families and compare it with the combined income of all 111 million households in the country, we see that the poorest 20 percent of households have only 3.4 percent of the total income. There are also 22 million households that earn more than $86,861, and they make up the richest 20 percent of all households. Their share of the total household income is a whopping 49.8 percent. Remember, there are the same number of households in the poorest and richest quintiles, but their shares of the total household income are dramatically different. The median household income, where half the households earn more and half the households earn less, was $43,300 in 2003.

The table also shows that the top 5 percent of households, earning above $154,120, account for 21.4 percent of the total income. Now,

Table 3.1   Distribution of Income of All Households, by Quintile, and Income of Highest-Paid Chief Executive Officers, in 2003

Income Quintile	Income Range	Percent of Total Income
Poorest 20%	$0–$17,984	3.4
Fourth 20%	17,985–34,000	8.7
Middle 20%	34,001–54,440	14.8
Second 20%	54,441–86,860	23.4
Top 20%	86,861 +	49.8
Richest 5%	154,120 +	21.4

Rank of Best-Paid CEOs	Individual Income	
400th (lowest-paid)	$1,500,000	
300th	$2,700,000	
200th	$4,200,000	
100th	$8,200,000	
1st (highest-paid)	$116,600,000	

Sources: US Census Bureau, *Income in the United States: 2003* (Washington, D.C.: US Department of Commerce), available at www.census.gov; *Forbes* 2003.

Note: The annual incomes of the poorest 20 percent of all households ranged from $0 to $17,984. The combined incomes of these 22 million households account for only 3.4 percent of the total income of all 111 million households combined. The median income of all households in the country was $43,300. Individual income of the CEOs is the total compensation they received from their companies. The individual CEO at the bottom of the list (no. 400) received $1.5 million in compensation in 2003.

$154,120 is not a bad income, but it pales in comparison with some of the incomes of people in the top 1 percent of households. *Forbes,* the business magazine promoted as "the capitalist's tool," collects information each year on the incomes of chief executive officers (CEOs) of the nation's largest corporations. This includes the total compensation from their companies but does not include other income they may have earned or the incomes of other family members.

As you can see at the bottom of Table 3.1, the four-hundredth best-paid CEO (Terry L. Shepard of St. Jude Medical) earned $1.5 million from his company, about thirty-five times higher than the median household income. But even this extraordinary income pales in comparison with the highest-paid CEO, Jeffrey C. Barbakow, who made $116.5 million in 2003. This staggering income of the CEO of Tenet Healthcare is 2,692 times higher than the median household income.

If we were to construct a graph of income inequality with each inch representing $100,000 of income, someone with the median household income would be about a half-inch above the floor. Terry Shepard, the poorest of the top 400 CEOs, would be fifteen inches from the floor. Jeffrey Barbakow would be ninety-six feet above the floor, on the ninth or tenth floor of an average building.

The gap between the salaries of CEOs and average workers has been growing rapidly. According to United for a Fair Economy (1999), CEOs made 42 times the salary of the average worker in 1980. By 1999, CEOs made 475 times more than the average worker. Using a slightly different methodology, the Economic Policy Institute estimates that the CEO/worker income gap increased from 24 times the salary in 1967 to 300 in 2000 (Mishel, Bernstein, and Allegretto 2005). Whichever data you prefer, economic inequality is increasing at an alarming rate.

This extraordinarily high level of income inequality is much greater than in Europe. According to World Bank data from the mid-1990s, the bottom income quintile in European industrialized countries accounted for 7–10 percent of the aggregate income, a much higher figure than in the United States. The top income quintiles in Europe accounted for 34–45 percent of the aggregate income, a much lower figure than in Europe (Hurst 2004; Kerbo 2003).

In addition, the CEOs in other industrialized countries earned substantially less than did American CEOs. French CEOs, for example, earned only 58 percent of the income of their American counterparts. In the United Kingdom, the comparable figure was 54 percent, in Germany it was 47 percent, and in Japan it was 44 percent (Kerbo 2003).

Just stating that income inequality exists is not sufficient. Another question is whether the degree of income inequality is growing, shrinking, or staying the same. Fortunately, the federal statistics allow us to examine this question. We have just discussed the share of aggregate household income that each quintile accounted for in 2003. These same data for other years are shown in Table 3.2.

As the table illustrates, the lowest quintile had a slightly *lower* proportion of the aggregate income in 2003 (3.4 percent) than in 1970 (4.1 percent). This means that the poor were worse off relative to everyone else in 2003 than they were in 1970. Looking at the households in the top 20 percent and the top 5 percent, the reverse is true. These better-off households have a *higher* proportion of the aggregate income in 2003 than they did in 1970. This means that the higher-income households are earning even higher incomes now than in the past while the lower-income households are losing ground. To put it another way, income inequality is getting worse. Incorporating the effect of taxes doesn't change this trend (Browning 2003).

As bad as income inequality is, wealth inequality is even worse. Table 3.3 shows the distribution of net worth in 2000. Fifteen percent of

Table 3.2   Share of Aggregate Household Income Received by
             Different Income Groups, 1970–2003

	Lowest 20% of Households	Highest 20% of Households	Top 5% of Households
2003	3.4%	49.8%	21.4%
2000	3.6	49.6	21.9
1990	3.9	46.6	18.6
1980	4.3	43.7	15.8
1970	4.1	43.3	16.6

Source: US Census Bureau, *Income in the United States: 2003* (Washington, D.C.: US Department of Commerce, 2003); available at www.census.gov.

Note: In 2003, the poorest 20 percent of households received only 3.4 percent of the aggregate income while the top 5 percent of households received 21.4 percent of the aggregate income.

Table 3.3   Distribution of Wealth (net worth) of All US Households in
             1991 and 2000 and Net Worth of the 400 Richest People in
             2004

All US Households	Percentage Distribution	
Net Worth	1991	2000
0 or negative	12.6%	15.0%
$1–4,999	14.2	9.2
$5,000–9,999	6.5	5.3
$10,000–24,999	11.2	8.4
$25,000–49,999	12.2	10.4
$50,999–99,999	15.1	14.1
$100,000–249,999	17.6	19.4
$250,000–499,999	7.0	10.1
$500,000 +	3.5	8.1

Richest 400 People in the United States, 2004	
Net Worth	Rank of Person
$750 million	400th
$1 billion	300th
$1.4 billion	200th
$2.1 billion	100th
$48 billion	1st (Bill Gates)

Source: US Census Bureau 1995, 2003b; Armstrong and Newcomb 2004.

Note: In 2000, 9.2 percent of all households had a net worth between $1 and $4,999. The median net worth was $46,506 in 2000 and $38,500 in 1991. In 2004, the 400th richest individual had a net worth of $750 million.

households had a zero or negative net worth, while 8.1 percent had a net worth of $500,000 or more. The median net worth was about $55,000.

When comparing the 2000 data with the 1991 data, it is clear that wealth inequality has gotten worse. The percentage of households with zero or negative net worth increased from 12.6 percent in 1991 to 15.0 percent in 2000. The number of households with a net worth of $500,000 or more also increased, from 3.5 percent in 1991 to 8.1 percent in 2000.

As we saw with income inequality, these data understate the true degree of wealth inequality. *Forbes* magazine also collects data on the 400 richest Americans (Armstrong and Newcomb 2004). The "poorest" people on the Forbes 400 list in 2004 (a twelve-way tie including Teresa Heinz Kerry, the wife of former Democratic presidential candidate Senator John Kerry) each have a net worth of $750 million. This is more than 13,000 times greater than the median net worth of all households. Three hundred twelve of the top 400 are billionaires. The net worth of the wealthiest person in the country, Bill Gates, is $48 *billion.* This is 64 times higher than the four-hundredth richest person and 873,000 times higher than the median family net worth. If we were to make a wealth graph that began on the first floor of a building wherein each inch would represent $100,000 of net worth, the median family net worth would be about one-half inch above the floor. Teresa Heinz Kerry and the other poorest people on the Forbes 400 list would be 625 feet from the floor, around the height of a sixty-story building. Bill Gates's net worth, in comparison, would be 40,000 *feet* from the bottom, above the cruising level of most jet airliners!

The federal government also collects data on poverty. The measure of poverty goes back to the 1960s, when it was assumed that families spend about one-third of their income on food. The US Department of Agriculture publishes an emergency food budget each year for different-sized families; the larger the family, the larger the food budget. The government takes this figure and multiplies it by three; the product becomes the official poverty threshold.

A family's before-tax money income includes wages, salaries, cash transfer payments like welfare, social security, and unemployment insurance. Capital gains and losses and the value of in-kind government services (e.g., food stamps, Medicaid, subsidized housing) are not included. This income is then compared with the poverty threshold. For a family of four, including two children, the poverty threshold was $18,810 in 2003. This means that if the family income were less than $18,810, those four people would be counted as among the poor. A three-person family with two children, in contrast, would have a poverty threshold of $14,680. If that family made $14,681 in 2003, they would not be considered to be poor. Using these calculations, 35.9 million people were counted as poor in 2003. This accounted for 12.5 percent of the US population.

Most poor adults work for at least part of the year. According to Yates (2005), almost one-quarter of all workers had such low hourly wages that they would still be poor even if they had worked year-round and full-time in 2003.

Some have argued that this measure is too generous and that it *overestimates* the number of poor people. Most important, many conservatives argue that the value of noncash in-kind government services (e.g., food stamps, subsidized housing and healthcare, etc.) should be *included as income*. They would also deduct income and payroll taxes and include the value of capital gains (of which the poor have virtually nothing). Keeping the same threshold levels, this revised measure reduces the poverty rate to only 9.4 percent of the population and eliminates 7.8 million people from the poverty count. These people have the same low incomes that they had by the previous measure; they are just not counted as poor anymore.

After looking at these numbers, we can return briefly to our discussions of class. The data show the limitations of the mainstream approach that doesn't deal with wealth and that stops at the highest quintile or decile of the income distribution. Someone with $185,000 in wealth just can't be in the same class as someone with billions. The Marxist approach, with its emphasis on wealth, can easily incorporate these figures by saying that these very wealthy people with high incomes are members of the capitalist class.

Finally, we will look at some numbers about social mobility, or the extent to which people move up and down the stratification system. In order to understand how a person's class origin affects his or her life, we look at intergenerational mobility by comparing a child's occupation with that of its parents. Traditionally this has meant looking at a son's occupation in comparison with his father's, although more recent studies have included women.

Gilbert (1998) compares the occupations of men and women 25–64 years of age in the 1980s with the occupations of their fathers. The first row of Table 3.4 looks only at the sons who had fathers with upper white-collar jobs. Sixty percent of these sons had upper white-collar jobs, which means that they were neither upwardly nor downwardly mobile. Only 14 percent of these sons had lower manual jobs, which is to say they were downwardly mobile.

The fourth row of the table looks only at the sons of fathers who had lower manual jobs. Only 27 percent of these sons had upper white-collar

Table 3.4   Comparison of Child's Occupation, 1982–1990, with Father's Occupation

	Son's Occupation (percentage)					
Father's Occupation	Upper White-Collar	Lower White-Collar	Upper Manual	Lower Manual	Farm	Total
Upper White-Collar	60%	14%	11%	14%	1%	100%
Lower White-Collar	39	18	19	23	1	100
Upper Manual	32	10	33	24	2	100
Lower Manual	27	11	25	37	1	100
Farm	19	10	22	33	16	100
Total (N = 4,632)	36	12	23	27	3	100
	Daughter's Occupation					
Upper White-Collar	51%	36%	2%	11%	0%	100%
Lower White-Collar	39	43	3	15	0	100
Upper Manual	27	45	3	25	0	100
Lower Manual	24	38	3	35	0	100
Farm	21	32	3	44	1	100
Total (N = 2,462)	32	39	3	27	0	100

Source: Gilbert 1998, 144, 146.

Notes: Upper White-Collar: professionals, managers, officials, nonretail sales; Lower White-Collar: proprietors, clerical, retail sales; Upper Manual: craftsmen and foremen; Lower Manual: service, operatives, nonfarm laborers; Farm: farmers and farm workers. Fifty-one percent of the daughters of white-collar fathers were themselves white-collar workers while only 24 percent of the daughters of lower manual fathers were themselves white-collar workers.

jobs, which means that they were upwardly mobile. In comparison, 37 percent of the sons had lower manual jobs, meaning they were not mobile.

These data show that while there is some upward and downward mobility among sons relative to their fathers, the sons of upper white-collar fathers were much more likely than the sons of lower manual fathers to have high-level jobs. Likewise, the sons of lower manual fathers were much more likely than the sons of upper white-collar fathers to have lower-level jobs.

The pattern for daughters relative to their fathers, shown in the bottom half of Table 3.4, is similar to the pattern for sons. The table also shows the low percentage of all daughters in the upper manual category (i.e., skilled blue-collar jobs). This is evidence of occupational sex segregation, which will be discussed at greater length in Chapter 5.

The *Economist* (2004), a mainstream British magazine, reviewed several recent studies and concluded that social mobility in the United States is declining:

A growing body of evidence suggests that the meritocratic ideal is in trouble in America. Income inequality is growing to levels not seen since the Gilded Age, around the 1880s. But social mobility is not increasing at anything like the same pace; would-be Horatio Algers are finding it no easier to climb from rags to riches, while the children of the privileged have a greater chance of staying at the top of the social heap. The United States risks calcifying into a European-style class-based society.

Though some upward mobility can be attributed to the superior work ethics of individual men and women, a lot of mobility is due to structural changes in the labor force. The number of people employed in farming has been declining for decades, so many of the children of farmers have to find nonfarm jobs. Also, white-collar occupations have been increasing faster than manual occupations, so that some of the children of lower manual workers are automatically "pushed up" in the occupational hierarchy.

These data show that while there is upward and downward mobility of children in terms of their own occupations relative to the occupations of their fathers, the best chance of getting into an upper white-collar occupation is to have a father in that occupation. In addition, most of the mobility consists of small steps between adjacent strata rather than big jumps from the bottom to the top. These findings are consistent with previous studies of social mobility. In addition, mobility rates in the United States are about the same as they are in other industrialized countries (Kerbo 2003; Beeghley 2005).

These data are somewhat limited in scope since upper white-collar occupations include teachers and lower-level managers as well as doctors and factory owners. It's one thing for the child of a factory worker to be a teacher, but it's quite another thing for the factory worker's child to become the owner of the factory.

There is also a certain amount of mobility among the wealthy. According to the Forbes 400 list of 2004, for example, forty-eight people had dropped off the list compared with the previous year, and forty-five new names were added. Of course, some of those who dropped off the list died, and others went from super-wealthy to very wealthy (like Michael Eisner of the Disney company). Most of the newcomers to the list, however, went from very wealthy to super-wealthy. One exception to this were the founders of Google, Sergey Brin and Larry Page. Their initial public stock offering made them instant billionaires.

A group called United for a Fair Economy (1997) analyzed the family origins of those people on the 1997 Forbes 400 list of the richest people in America. UFFE used a baseball analogy of starting in the batters' box and ending up on home plate. It found that 43 percent of the Forbes 400 started out on home plate; that is, they inherited enough wealth—at least $475 million in 1997—to be on the list without doing anything (e.g., J. Paul Getty Jr. and David Rockefeller). Another 7 percent were born on third base—they inherited at least $50 million, so they had to work to increase their wealth in order to get on the list (e.g., Kenneth Feld and Walter Annenberg). Six percent were born on second base by inheriting a small company and/or wealth of more than $1 million (e.g., Donald Tyson and Frank Purdue). Fourteen percent were born on first base by being born into a prominent family but didn't inherit more than $1 million (e.g., Bill Gates). That left 30 percent who began in the batters' box, meaning that their families didn't have great wealth (e.g., H. Ross Perot and John Werner Kluge). However, even most of those who began in the batters' box did not come from poor or working-class families. If you want to be rich, your best chance is to be born into a rich family.

▨ Prejudice and Ideology

Most mainstream commentators would argue that the United States is a middle-class society, implying that most Americans are middle-class. As we saw in the previous section, however, there is no agreement on how class should be measured. In addition, Americans are not consistent in terms of how they identify their own class position.

In 2005, a *New York Times*/CBS News poll asked a national sample of adults to indicate which of five social classes they belonged to. The results are as follows:

1 percent – upper class
15 percent – upper-middle class
42 percent – middle class
35 percent – working class
7 percent – lower class

Although a majority saw themselves as middle-class, more than two-fifths of the population did not (*New York Times*/CBS News 2005).

Ladd and Bowman (1998) review the literature on how Americans see themselves in national public opinion surveys over time. Although different surveys ask different questions, it is clear that a substantial proportion of the population has always identified themselves as working-class. The National Opinion Research Center, for example, asked the same question as the *New York Times*/CBS News poll but without the "upper-middle class" option. When the question was first asked in 1949, 61 percent identified themselves with the working class and only 32 percent with the middle class. Between 1972 and 1983, respondents were slightly more likely to identify with the working class rather than the middle class. Since 1984, however, respondents have tended to be more likely to identify with the middle class than with the working class. When given a chance, then, a substantial portion of Americans have always seen themselves as members of the working class, not the middle class.

Another aspect of the middle-class society ethos is the connection between hard work and economic success. Ladd and Bowman show that this has been an enduring belief among most Americans. In a 1952 survey, for example, respondents were asked the following: "Some people say there's not much opportunity in America today—that the average man doesn't have much chance to really get ahead. Others say there's plenty of opportunity, and anyone who works hard can go as far as he wants. How do you feel about this?" (quoted in Ladd and Bowman 1998, 54). Eighty-seven percent said that there was opportunity, and 8 percent said that there was only little opportunity.

Unfortunately, the question was asked differently in different years. In 1997, the true-false question was phrased this way: "People who work hard in this nation are likely to succeed" (Ladd and Bowman 1998, 55). Seventy-nine percent of the respondents said this was true, and only 18 percent said it was false.

The *New York Times*/CBS News poll (2005) asked how important various qualities are for "getting ahead in life." Eighty-seven percent said that hard work was "essential" or "very important" for getting ahead. Having a good education was almost as important, at 85 percent. This was followed by having natural ability (71 percent), knowing the right people (48 percent), and coming from a wealthy family (44 percent). Although it is not possible to compare all these surveys since the questions are different, Americans clearly still believe strongly in the work ethic.

The flip side of the work-success question concerns explanations for poverty. The following question was put to national samples between 1964 and 1997: "In your opinion, which is more often to blame if a person is poor—lack of effort on his own part, or circumstances beyond his control?" (Ladd and Bowman 1998, 52). In 1964, 35 percent said that lack of effort was the cause of poverty and 29 percent said poverty was caused by circumstances. The remaining 32 percent said both were responsible. This means that two-thirds of the population thought that lack of effort was either partially or completely the cause of poverty (Ladd and Bowman 1998). This is sometimes called the "blame the victim" explanation of poverty since the cause is located within poor individuals.

By 1997, responses had become more polarized. Forty-four percent blamed circumstances, 39 percent blamed lack of effort, and only 14 percent said both. Slightly more than half of the respondents still felt that lack of effort was a partial or complete explanation of poverty, a substantial decline from 1964. Americans tend to agree that hard work brings success, but they are divided on what causes poverty.

The belief that poverty is caused by some cultural defect in the poor themselves is one of the enduring beliefs in American culture and social science. In the 1960s, anthropologist Oscar Lewis coined the phrase "culture of poverty." This term has gone through a variety of changes, with one of the more recent simply referring to *the cultural explanation of poverty* (Harrison 1992). The argument put forward by conservative scholars is that some substantial proportion of poor people have cultural values, passed on from one generation to the next, that cause them to be noncompetitive in the modern labor force. The components of this culture are said to be living in the present rather than planning for the future, feelings of powerlessness, broken families and confused gender roles, a proclivity for deviant behavior, and a dependence on welfare.

According to this view, then, poverty is caused by the attitudes of poor people themselves, not by circumstances beyond their control, such as economic recession, racial discrimination, globalization, or the actions of the capitalist class. The solution is to change their culture, not to provide more opportunities. The assumption is that substantial opportunities are there for the taking. Clearly, the thrust of this book is inconsistent with the culture of poverty analysis. Cultural differences cannot explain the growing income and wealth inequality that we discussed earlier.

Americans are certainly aware of the inequality that exists in the United States, although they seem to have ambivalent attitudes about it. The most recent polls show that while they admire people who got rich through hard work (89 percent) and think that the country benefits from having a class of rich people (62 percent), they don't think it's likely that they will become rich (61 percent). They also think that the rich don't pay their fair share of taxes (72 percent) and that the tax system is unfair to working people (74 percent). In addition, 76 percent agreed with the statement "The rich are getting richer and the poor are getting poorer" (Ladd and Bowman 1998).

In spite of these beliefs about the unfairness of economic inequality, Ladd and Bowman (1998) provide data showing that Americans disagree on whether and how the government should respond to income inequality. Using a seven-point scale, respondents were asked to use a score of 1 to indicate their belief that the government should reduce income differences by raising taxes on the wealthy and giving income assistance to the poor. A score of 7 would indicate that the government should not concern itself with income inequality.

When the question was first asked in 1973, 48 percent said that the government should try to reduce inequality and 22 percent said that they shouldn't. The remaining 27 percent were in between. In the relatively liberal early 1970s, almost half of the population was sympathetic to government action to reduce inequality.

By 1996, however, things had changed dramatically. Only 28 percent said that the government should decrease inequality, a substantial drop from 1973. Twenty percent said that the government shouldn't decrease inequality, a small drop from 1973. Fifty percent were now in the middle, a sharp rise from 1973. During the conservative 1990s, there was considerably less enthusiasm for government action to reduce inequality.

Not surprisingly, people from different income levels had different attitudes about government action. In 1996, 32 percent of survey respondents with family incomes of less than $20,000 thought that the government should act to reduce inequality, but only 20 percent of those with incomes of $50,000 or more felt this way. However, though only 12 percent of respondents with low incomes thought that the government should not take action, 38 percent of the high-income respondents felt this way. From the 1970s to the 1990s, low-income support for government action remained stable, but high-income support dropped.

The results of these national surveys do not show an American population that is united over the theme of middle-class America. It shows a population with differing viewpoints, depending on where they are in the system of inequality.

■ Discrimination and Capitalism

Since the 1970s, capitalism has not been kind to working people. Although there have been a variety of corporate scandals in the first years of the twenty-first century that have hurt working people in a variety of ways, it is the legal workings of capitalism that are the larger problem.

In the previous chapter I introduced the concept of discrimination and defined it as *actions that deny equal treatment to persons perceived to be members of some social category or group.* As we will see in the following chapters, I will show how the dominant groups (i.e., whites, men, and heterosexuals) still practice intentional discrimination in terms of race, gender, and sexual orientation in a variety of ways (e.g., employment, housing, education, etc.). Sometimes this discrimination is at the individual level, and sometimes it is institutional. Sometimes it is illegal, and sometimes it isn't.

Even so, the concept of discrimination doesn't adequately describe the nature of class domination. The capitalist class has power over other classes and can live in neighborhoods and go to restaurants that working-class people can't, but this usually doesn't involve unequal treatment due to membership in a certain category, and there is usually nothing illegal about it. A secretary can't buy a home in Beverly Hills because he or she can't afford it. A restaurant can refuse service to people who can't pay its prices. Most families can't afford private schools, so they send their kids to public schools. A factory owner has the legal right to hire and fire workers and to boss them around. A wealthy political candidate can legally outspend a middle-class opponent by using millions of his or her own personal fortune to win an election. These and other policies, which are certainly unfair, are built into the capitalist system. The concept of discrimination doesn't capture the essence of this type of unfairness. Exploitation, where *the dominant group uses the subordinate group for its own ends*, seems closer to the truth.

Increasingly, capitalism has become a global economic system. Private corporations and their national governments have always tried to look outside their borders for raw materials, new markets, and cheap labor. This goes back to the seventeenth and eighteenth centuries, when European countries established colonies around the world.

With the development of rapid transportation, more sophisticated production techniques, and the information technology explosion, globalization has taken a great leap forward. Huge multinational corporations operate around the world, and their country of origin has become less important. Corporations move their operations to areas of the world that offer cheaper labor costs, lower taxes, and fewer environmental regulations. Countries compete with one another in what some have called *the race to the bottom* (Zweig 2000).

This causes real problems for working people in the United States and other industrialized countries due to their relatively high wages compared with workers in the developing world. It's often cheaper for American companies to have their products assembled in Third World countries and ship them to the United States than to pay American workers to do the work. It's impossible for American workers to compete with workers in China or El Salvador who make only a few dollars per day. According to some estimates, the United States lost as many as 1 million jobs between 2000 and 2004.

This has resulted in a phenomenon known as "displaced workers." According to the Bureau of Labor Statistics (2002), displaced workers are "persons 20 years of age and older who lost or left jobs because their plant or company closed or moved, there was insufficient work for them to do, or their position or shift was abolished." Between January 1999 and December 2001, the BLS estimates that as many as 10 million workers were displaced.

The BLS then surveyed displaced workers who had been with their employer at least three years prior to displacement. At the time of the survey, only 64 percent of these workers had found new jobs, 21 percent were unemployed, and 15 percent had dropped out of the labor force. Of those who were reemployed, over half were earning less than what they had earned on the job they lost. Twenty-nine percent of them had income losses of 20 percent or more. In other words, the majority of displaced workers had become downwardly mobile (also see Helwig 2004).

When most of us think of displaced workers, we probably think of factory workers in the steel, auto, rubber, or textile industries. Indeed, almost one-fifth of the workers in the survey were operators, fabricators, or laborers. But 30 percent were professional and managerial workers, and 29 percent were technical, sales, and administrative support workers.

Increasing numbers of American corporations "outsource" some of their work to companies in Ireland, India, and other low-wage countries. In India, a company named WIPRO employs 30,000 people who handle frequent-flyer issues for airlines, customer service complaints from retail sales stores, and even the interpretation of X-rays taken in US hospitals (Rai 2004). The relentless search for lower labor costs to increase profits is costing working people good jobs. Americans often blame Indian or Chinese workers for "taking their jobs," but it is the profit-oriented corporations that are truly to blame.

Globalization is also a contributing factor to the decline of labor unions in the United States. In 1955, more than one-third of the labor force belonged to a union. In 2003, that figure had plummeted to 13 percent. This is much lower than other countries in the industrialized world. More than one-fourth of Japanese workers and 42 percent of workers in England are unionized (Zweig 2000; Kerbo 2003). The decline in the American manufacturing industries, many of which were unionized, is one reason for the drop in union membership. Now, government workers, including teachers, are much more likely to be unionized (37 percent) than workers in the private sector (8 percent).

Without unions, working people cannot negotiate effectively with employers for wages, benefits, and working conditions. According to Yates (2005), unionized workers earn 15 percent more than nonunion workers after controlling for factors such as education, work experience, and age. The decline in unionization has contributed to the growth in income inequality. However, even unionized workers have had a difficult time holding on to hard-fought gains.

Another structural issue is the types of jobs that are available in the United States. According to popular knowledge, high-skilled, high-paying jobs are displacing lower-skilled, low-paying jobs because of high-tech industries. The reality, as we shall see, is considerably more complex.

Every two or three years, the Bureau of Labor Statistics revs up its computers and does a ten-year projection of which jobs will grow and which won't. The most recent projections are for the period 2002–2012 (Hecker 2004). The data in Table 3.5 show the occupations that are expected to produce the most new jobs by 2012. Registered nurses and postsecondary teachers top the list and are expected to add 623,000 and 603,000 new jobs, respectively. This is certainly consistent with the popular view that more and more jobs require education beyond high school. However, the next five occupations on the list require only modest skills—retail sales, customer service, fast food, cashiers, and janitors. In fact, seven of the ten occupations that are expected to add the most new jobs by 2012 are in the lower two income quartiles and only require on-the-job training!

Where are the high-tech computer jobs that everyone has been talking about since the 1980s? How do we reconcile this list with the belief that most jobs these days require high levels of education? Well, let's consider another list.

The data in Table 3.6 show the ten *fastest-growing* jobs. Here we find three computer-related occupations. Systems and data communication analysts are projected to increase by 57 percent, and two types of computer software engineers are projected to increase by 45–46 percent. All three of these computer-related jobs are in the top income quartile and require a college education. Physicians' assistants are also on the list. However, the fastest-growing job is that of medical assistant, which is projected to grow by 59 percent. This is in the next-to-lowest income quartile and requires moderate on-the-job training. Even this list contains both skilled, high-paying jobs and lower-skilled, lower-paying jobs.

**Table 3.5   Occupations Projected to Add the Most New Jobs,
2002–2012**

Occupational Category	Employment in 2002 (thousands)	New Jobs by 2012 (thousands)	Percent Change	Income Quartile[a]	Qualifications/ Training
Registered nurses	2,284	**623**	27%	1	AA
Postsecondary teachers	1,581	**603**	38	1	PhD
Retail salespersons	4,076	**596**	15	4	Short-term OJT[b]
Customer service rep	1,894	**460**	24	3	Moderate-term OJT
Food preparation and serving workers, including fast food	1,990	**454**	23	4	Short-term OJT
Cashiers, except gaming	3,432	**454**	13	4	Short-term OJT
Janitors and cleaners	2,267	**414**	18	4	Short-term OJT
General and operations managers	2,049	**376**	18	1	BA or higher plus experience
Waiters and waitresses	2,097	**367**	18	4	Short-term OJT
Nursing aides, orderlies, attendants	1,375	**343**	25	3	Short-term OJT

Source: Hecker 2004.
Notes: a. 1 = highest annual income quartile ($41,820 and over); 4 = lowest quartile (below $19,600).
b. OJT = on-the-job training.

For those who find this all confusing, let me explain. Table 3.5 identifies large occupations that are growing at modest rates. There were 2.3 million registered nurses employed in 2002; this number is expected to grow by 623,000 by 2012, resulting in a growth rate of 27 percent. Only 365,000 people were employed as medical assistants in 2002, the top job on the fastest-growing list of Table 3.6. This relatively small occupation is projected to expand by 59 percent, an increase in 215,000 jobs. The three computer-related occupations are also relatively small in number.

What does this mean? For the next decade or two, there will still be more openings for retail sales, customer service, and food preparation workers than for systems analysts, computer software engineers, and physicians' assistants. There will be more jobs for cashiers and janitors than for registered nurses. A college degree in the right major increases

Table 3.6 Occupations Projected to Have the Fastest Growth Rates, 2002–2012

Occupational Category	Employment in 2002 (thousands)	New Jobs by 2012 (thousands)	**Percent Change**	Income Quartile[a]	Qualifications/ Training
Medical assistants	365	215	**59**	3	Moderate-term OJT[b]
Systems and data communication analysts	186	106	**57**	1	BA
Physicians' assistants	63	31	**49**	1	BA
Social and human service assistants	305	149	**49**	3	Moderate-term OJT
Home health aides	580	279	**48**	4	Short-term OJT
Medical records and health information techs	147	69	**47**	3	AA
Physical therapist aides	37	17	**46**	3	Short-term OJT
Computer software engineers, applications	394	179	**46**	1	BA
Computer software engineers, systems software	281	128	**45**	1	BA
Physical therapist assistants	50	22	**45**	2	AA

Source: Hecker 2004.
Notes: a. 1 = highest annual income quartile ($41,820 and over); 4 = lowest quartile (below $19,600).
b. OJT = on-the-job training.

one's chances of getting one of the better-paying jobs, but there are more college graduates than college-level jobs. This means that the job structure provides opportunities for upward mobility for some college graduates, but also restricts these opportunities for others.

Another barrier to upward mobility is what some have called the Wal-Mart Revolution (Walker 2004). The statistics are astonishing. In 2003, Wal-Mart had sales of $247 billion, making it the world's largest company based on sales. It had higher sales than International Business Machines, Coca-Cola, Time Warner, and Microsoft combined. Comparing this figure to the gross domestic product of industrialized countries, Wal-Mart would be the nineteenth-largest country, just below Belgium and above Sweden. Wal-Mart had over $9 billion in profits in 2003 and employed 1.3 million people in the United States and ten other countries.

There are more than 3,200 Wal-Mart stores in the United States and another 1,000 or so around the world. Wal-Mart controls 15 percent of

US grocery sales, and the company is trying for 30 percent. It sells more than 20 percent of all Dial, Clorox, and Revlon products. Its sales account for 2 percent of the gross domestic product of the United States.

The secret to Wal-Mart's success is high volume and low labor costs, which result in low prices. Most Wal-Mart employees work part-time with no benefits. The average wage is $7.50–$8.50 an hour, 20–30 percent less than at Target and Kmart. The average worker earns $18,000 per year, which is around the poverty level for a family of four. Needless to say, Wal-Mart is aggressively anti-union. Early in the twentieth century, Henry Ford tried to keep wages low, but he understood that he had to pay his assembly-line workers sufficient wages that they could buy the cars they produced. Wal-Mart doesn't even pay enough for a family head to provide enough food for his or her family. This is an example of economic exploitation.

Wal-Mart has such power that it suppresses wages in the communities where it has stores. Smaller chains find it difficult to compete with Wal-Mart, and local businesses find it almost impossible. Wal-Mart also drives hard bargains with the manufacturers of the products it sells. By insisting on the lowest possible prices, Wal-Mart is practically forcing manufacturers to move to China, where labor costs are extremely low. This, of course, means fewer jobs for Americans. To the extent that Wal-Mart becomes the business model of the future, working people are going to be in trouble.

Conclusion

I hope that readers now feel more familiar with the current nature of class in the United States. Although we are a class-based society, we don't usually talk about class. As I stated at the beginning of this chapter, I have purposely stayed away from looking at how race, gender, and sexual orientation are intertwined with class. I made this decision because I wanted to emphasize class inequalities without getting sidetracked into a discussion of race and gender inequality. In Chapter 4, however, I will discuss race and try to show how class is integral to understanding racial conflict. I also hope to show how race is integral to understanding class conflict.

4

Race

RACIAL CONFLICT AND INEQUALITY IS STILL ONE OF THE MAJOR issues facing the United States in the twenty-first century. A century ago, W. E. B. DuBois (1990, 3) wrote, "The problem of the 20th Century is the problem of the color line." This is still true in the twenty-first century.

When DuBois wrote those words, white supremacy over blacks was the main issue. In the twenty-first century, however, this bipolar model is no longer adequate. US Census Bureau (2004) figures show that the Hispanic population has surpassed the black population and that the Asian population is growing rapidly. Census Bureau projections suggest that sometime in the 2050s, non-Hispanic whites may cease to be the numerical majority. Most social science research has not caught up to these changing demographics and is still stuck in the bipolar model.

Readers may wonder why it is necessary to talk about "non-Hispanic whites" rather than just "whites." Are there also non-Hispanic blacks or Asians? What about the mixed-race population? Before answering these and other questions, it is necessary to define some basic terms.

▨ Terminology

Although many of us assume that we know what race means, it's really not so simple. Before proceeding, try writing out a definition and you'll find out what I mean. For the purposes of this book, a **racial group** *is* *a social group that is socially defined as having certain biological char-acteristics that set them apart from other groups, often in invidious ways.* The key aspect of this definition is that race is defined socially, not biologically.

Many people don't realize that most biologists and geneticists argue that race is not a biologically meaningful term. Of course there are clear observable, biological differences between some groups of people in terms of skin color, hair texture, facial shapes, and so on. However, when one examines the genetic makeup of people from different races, there is more genetic variation within a given race than between races. In other words, the genes for skin color and for a few other observable characteristics may be different, but most everything else is the same.

It's also impossible to tell where one race stops and another begins. Speaking in the excellent video *Race: The Power of an Illusion* (2003), evolutionary biologist Joseph Graves Jr. puts it this way:

> If we were to only look at people in the tropics and people in Norway, we would come to the conclusion that there is a group of people who have light skin and a group of people who have dark skin. But, if we were to walk from the tropics to Norway, what we would see is a continuous change in skin tones. At no point during that trip would we be able to say, "Oh, this is the place in which we go from the dark race to the light race."

Although race is not a valid biological concept, it is still a powerful cultural concept, especially in the United States. We *think* race is important, and we *treat* people in different ways according to the race we think they belong to. In other words, we have socially constructed racial categories even though they have no biological significance. Consequently, our approaches to race are often illogical and inconsistent.

In trying to determine who is black, Americans have generally used the "one drop" rule. People are considered black if they have any black ancestors, regardless of the color of their skin. In the past, this has been encoded into law. In more recent years, it's simply part of the culture. Some light-skinned people with black ancestors can be "mistaken" for being white if no one knows the history of their family. This phenomenon of **passing** *refers to a subordinate group member who does not reveal the stigmatized status that he or she occupies.* If the secret is revealed, the person previously defined as white, for example, becomes redefined as black.

Contrast this with how Native Americans are defined through their "blood quantum." If you have a Native American mother and a white father, you are considered to be "half Indian." If one of your grandparents was a Native American and the other three were not, you are one-fourth Indian. Individual tribes can define the blood quantum level that is necessary to be a member of the tribe. This can range from being half Indian to being one-fourth Indian to simply self-identifying as Indian. In contradistinction to the one-drop rule for blacks, Native Americans have to prove that they are Indian enough to be a member of the tribe. The federal government requires that people be at least one-fourth Indian to qualify for programs sponsored by the Bureau of Indian Affairs.

The census data on race that I mentioned earlier are totally unscientific since they are based on people's self-identification. That is, individuals are asked to check one of the boxes in the question on race—white, black, Asian, Pacific Islander, Native American, or "Some Other Race." However, none of the boxes say "Hispanic" because the census defines being Hispanic as an ethnicity, not as a race. Respondents first are asked whether they are Hispanic and then are asked to indicate their race. This means that Hispanics can be of any race.

An **ethnic group** is defined as *a social group that has certain cultural characteristics that set them off from other groups and whose members see themselves as having a common past.* Language and culture, according to the census, are what set Hispanics off from other groups (although Brazilians are classified as Hispanic in spite of the fact that they speak Portuguese). Arab Americans would also be an ethnic group for the same reason.

This race-versus-ethnicity issue becomes both interesting and problematic in trying to answer a simple question like "What percentage of the population is white?" The top half of Table 4.1 presents the data using the five standard racial categories plus a mixed-race category. Out of the 290.8 million Americans in 2003, 234.1 million were white, which accounts for 80.5 percent of the population. Reading down the columns, we can see that 12.8 percent of the population were black, 4.1 percent were Asian, 1 percent were Native American, 0.2 percent were Pacific Islanders, and 1.5 percent were mixed race. In addition, 13.7 percent of the population was Hispanic. If all these numbers are added together, they come out to 113.7 percent, and the total population comes to 330.7 million! What's going on here? The problem is that since Hispanics can be of any race, they are counted twice. A white Hispanic would be counted once as a white and once as a Hispanic. The categories are not mutually exclusive.

Table 4.1   Race/Ethnic Distribution of the US Population in 2003

Race/Ethnic Group	Number (millions)	Percent
White	234.1	80.5%
Black	37.1	12.8
Asian	11.9	4.1
American Indian/Alaskan	2.8	1.0
Hawaiian/Pacific Islander	0.5	0.2
Two or more races	4.3	1.5
Total	290.8	100.0
Hispanic (any race)	39.9	13.7
Total	330.7	113.7

Race/Ethnic Group	Number (millions)	Percent
Non-Hispanic		
White	197.3	67.8%
Black	35.6	12.2
Asian	11.7	4.0
American Indian/Alaskan	2.2	0.7
Hawaiian/Pacific Islander	0.4	0.1
Two or more races	3.7	1.3
Total	250.9	86.1
Hispanic	39.9	13.7
Total	290.8	100.0

Source: US Census Bureau 2004.

A second way to answer the question can be found in the bottom half of Table 4.1, which separates Hispanics and non-Hispanics. In this case, there are 197.3 million non-Hispanic whites, accounting for 67.8 percent of the population. The white category lost 36.8 million people since they were placed in the Hispanic category. The percentages for the other racial categories also decreased some. The total non-Hispanic population is 250.9 million, or 86.1 percent of the population. The Hispanic number (39.9 million, or 13.7 percent) is the same in both halves of the table. Most Hispanics are white, although others are from different races. This time, the total adds up to 290.8 million and 100 percent. The categories in the lower half of Table 4.1 are mutually exclusive in that everyone is only counted once.

So, are whites 80.5 percent of the population, or 67.8 percent of the population? Actually, both are correct. If ethnicity is ignored and all those who check the white box are counted, whites are 80.5 percent of the population. If only whites who are not also Hispanics are counted, non-Hispanic whites are 67.8 percent of the population. Sometimes federal officials use one number, and sometimes they use the other.

I will use the "non-Hispanic white" category when the data are available because it makes it easier to see the advantages that whites have in terms of income, occupation, and education. The gaps between non-Hispanic whites and people of color are usually larger than the gaps between all whites and people of color.

But wait, there's more. Remember the "some other race" category? In the 2000 census, 42 percent of Hispanics checked this box since they didn't think they fit into any of the standard race categories. In fact, most people who check "some other race" are Hispanic. This really upset census officials. Because some government agencies use the Modified Age/Race and Sex File (MARS), which doesn't include the "other" category, census officials must reassign those who select "some other race" to one of the standard categories. This creates many errors as well as a lot of extra work. In order to "encourage" Hispanics to select one of the standard racial categories, census officials are considering eliminating the "some other race" category for the 2010 census. This, in turn, provoked the following comment from Carlos Chardon, chair of the Census Bureau's Hispanic Advisory Committee: "We don't fit into the categories that the Anglos want us to fit in. The census is trying to create a reality that doesn't exist" (Swarns 2004, A18). The drama continues.

If this wasn't bad enough, there is the issue of how to deal with mixed-race people. Professional golfer Tiger Woods is usually described as black even though he is half Asian. After the conservative southern senator Strom Thurmond died in 2003, a dark-skinned woman revealed that she was his daughter. In his youth, Thurmond fathered a daughter by having a relationship with one of his black servants. The daughter, however, is always described as black even though she is half white.

Prior to the 2000 census, there was a big controversy over how to deal with mixed-race people. In previous years, a person who is half Asian and half Native American had to select only one box. Some biracial people argued for a separate "mixed race" category on the 2000 census because those from more than one racial background share a variety of similar issues. The final decision, however, was to allow people to check more than one box. In fact, 1.5 million Americans made that choice. The mixed-race–versus–multiple box issue had absolutely nothing to do with biology.

In addition to language and national origin, an ethnic group can be characterized by religion, especially if it is not the dominant religion.

The more than 5 million Muslims in America can be referred to as an ethnic group. It is important not to equate being Muslim with being Arab. Arabic language and culture are very prevalent in North Africa and the Middle East, although Iran and Turkey are not Arab countries. The dominant language in Iran is Farsi, and the dominant language in Turkey is Turkish. However, these two countries are Muslim countries in terms of the dominant religion. There are about 1.2 billion Muslims in the world, most of whom are not Arabs. There are over 300 million Arabs in the world, most of whom are Muslim. To make matters even more confusing, most of the 3 million Arab Americans are Christian (*Detroit Free Press* 2001; American-Arab Anti-Discrimination Committee 2002). If that isn't confusing enough, the census defines people from North Africa as white!

Jewish Americans are also an ethnic group, although there are important cultural differences among them. Ashkenazi Jews originally came from central and eastern Europe whereas Sephardic Jews came from Spain and Northern Africa. The vernacular language for Ashkenazi Jews was Yiddish, and the vernacular for Sephardic Jews was Ladino. There are also differences in rituals and holiday celebrations.

Most Jews are religious and belong to one of the four major denominations—orthodox, conservative, reform, and reconstructionist. However, there are also many people who define themselves as Jews culturally, but who are not religious. In fact, 80 percent of Jews in Israel are secular. In the United States, there are two national secular Jewish organizations—the Congress of Secular Jewish Organizations, and Secular Humanist Judaism (Seid 2001).

Technically, Protestants and Catholics are also ethnic groups by virtue of their religions, but they are not usually referred to this way because Christianity is the dominant religion in the United States. Ethnicity usually refers to groups that are culturally different from the dominant group or groups.

Now we get to the really big concept—racism. Believe it or not, there is no commonly accepted definition of this widely used term. Some social scientists use the term synonymously with *prejudice* in terms of one person having a negative attitude about someone from another group. Others see racism as the same thing as *discrimination* (i.e., differential treatment). In an often-cited article, Bob Blauner (1992) argues that there are at least four additional uses of the term.

The most useful definition of **racism** is *a system of oppression based on race*. According to this view, racism involves the power of one group to oppress another group. Racism, then, is systemic; it doesn't just exist in the minds of individuals. Joe Feagin (2000, 6), for example, states, "Systemic racism includes the complex array of antiblack practices, the unjustly gained political-economic power of whites, the continuing economic and other resource inequalities along racial lines, and the white racist ideologies and attitudes created to maintain and rationalize white privilege and power."

Although this definition of racism may seem straightforward, it has some important and controversial implications. Since racism involves power and oppression, it follows that only the dominant group can be racist. In the United States, this means that only whites can be racist. People of color cannot be racist because they don't have the power. Many whites strenuously object to this argument and say, "I know plenty of people of color who hate whites." True enough, there are people of color who are *prejudiced*. However, people of color are not *racist* because they lack the collective power to oppress whites as a group.

Others have argued that "all whites are racist." If what is meant by this statement is that all whites are prejudiced, this is certainly not the case, as we will discuss shortly. If what is meant is that all whites discriminate against people of color, this is also not the case. Many whites don't have the power to discriminate. If, however, what is meant is that whites participate in an oppressive system that benefits them, this comes closer to the truth. One group of whites who are committed to fighting against white racism goes so far as to describe themselves as "antiracists" rather than "nonracists." They agree with the argument that all whites are racist in that they participate in a racist system, but see themselves as trying to fight for a more equal world (O'Brien 2001). We will discuss these issues in the rest of this chapter.

Finally, there is the issue of the terminology to use when referring to different race and ethnic groups. Once again, there is no scientific answer here. The issue of "labels" is a contentious one that changes over time. It also involves how groups are labeled by outsiders versus how groups refer to themselves. In attempts to politically mobilize, subordinate groups often adopt new labels.

At various times in American history, it was considered appropriate by both blacks and whites to call blacks "colored" or "Negro." The National Association of Colored People (NAACP) was founded as an integrated antiracist organization in 1909. Martin Luther King Jr. used *Negro* in most of his speeches. Blacks in general do not like these terms today. In the 1960s, the term *black* replaced *Negro*. That was followed by *Afro-American* and *African American*. A 1995 poll of black Americans showed that 44 percent preferred "black," 28 percent preferred

"African American," and 12 percent preferred "Afro-American." Only 3 percent said "Negro" and 1 percent said "colored" (Infoplease 2004).

Some blacks from Africa and the Caribbean prefer to call themselves Nigerian, Kenyan, Haitian, or Jamaican. In addition to reflecting their country of origin, these labels can be an attempt to shield themselves from the racism experienced by American-born blacks. African and Caribbean blacks sometimes cultivate their distinctive accents in order to make themselves more attractive to potential employers who may discriminate against American-born blacks. While this strategy may have some short-term positive impact, the American-born children of immigrants usually lose their accents and are seen as black.

What about pejorative terms such as *nigger, chink,* and *spic*? On the one hand, *nigger* has been such a powerful negative term throughout American history that many whites and blacks can't even say it out loud. Instead, they talk about "the n-word." On the other hand, some blacks use the term *niggah* to refer approvingly to each other but would consider it offensive if whites used the same term. This is an example of a subordinate group taking a term of approbation and turning it on its head. Although this may be confusing to whites, the safest thing is to stay away from *nigger* and *niggah,* as well as any other pejorative racial terms (Akom 2000).

The term *Hispanic* was adopted by Congress in the 1970s to categorize a diverse set of people who share a common language. Previously, this population usually referred to themselves by their country of origin; for example, Cuban, Guatemalan, or Colombian. *Latino,* a term preferred by some political activists, also refers to Spanish-heritage populations. In a 1995 study (Infoplease 2004), 58 percent of those surveyed preferred "Hispanic," 12 percent preferred "Spanish Origin," and 12 percent preferred "Latino." In the southwestern United States, Mexican Americans sometimes refer to themselves as "Chicano."

The terms *Native American* and *American Indian* are both used to describe people who are descendants of indigenous people. In the same 1995 study, half preferred "American Indian," and 37 percent preferred "Native American."

Prior to the 1960s, most people from Asia and the Pacific Islands referred to themselves by their or their ancestors' country of origin. During the 1960s, however, Asian student activists started promoting the term *Asian* as a way of unifying people for political purposes (Espiritu 1992). The 1995 study discussed earlier did not mention Asians. It did, however, ask what whites like to be called. Sixty-two percent said "white" and 17 percent said "Caucasian."

This issue of labeling may seem trivial and arbitrary to members of dominant groups, but it's not. Often, when a subordinate group is beginning to mobilize to fight oppression, the ability to label itself is part of the process. When the Black Power movement split off from the civil rights movement in the 1960s, for example, activists insisted on being called "black" rather than "Negro."

◼ Descriptive Statistics

Virtually all the data collected by the federal government show substantial economic inequalities between whites and people of color. People are counted as unemployed if they don't have a job and are actively looking for work. Being in the labor force means that you are working or you are looking for work. Discouraged workers are not counted because they are viewed as having dropped out of the labor force. The unemployment rate is calculated as follows:

$$\frac{\text{no. looking for work}}{\text{no. working} + \text{no. looking for work}} = \% \text{ unemployed.}$$

The data in Table 4.2 show that unemployment rates in 2004 ranged from 4.4 percent for Asians and 4.8 percent for whites to 10.4 percent for blacks and 7.0 percent for Hispanics. The black unemployment rate is more than twice as high as the white rate and has been that way for

Table 4.2   Unemployment Rates for Sixteen-Year-Olds and Older in 2004, by Race, Spanish Origin, and Gender

Race/Spanish Origin	Male (%)	Female (%)	Total (%)
White	5.0[a]	4.7	4.8
Black	11.1	9.8	10.4
Asian	4.5	4.3	4.4
Hispanic	6.5	7.6	7.0
Black/white	2.2[b]	2.1	2.2
Asian/white	0.9	0.9	1.2
Hispanic/white	1.3	1.8	1.5

Source: http://www.bls.gov/cps.
Notes: a. E.g., 5.0 percent of white males were unemployed in 2004.
b. E.g., the black male unemployment rate was 2.2 times higher than the white male rate.

decades. The Department of Labor has only recently begun to collect data on Asians and Hispanics.

One common explanation for the difference between whites and Asians, on the one hand, and blacks and Hispanics, on the other hand, looks to education. Because low education leads to high unemployment and since blacks and Hispanics have lower levels of education than whites, the argument goes, it's not unreasonable to expect that there should be differences in unemployment. An extension of this argument is that at the same level of education, unemployment rates for whites, blacks, and Hispanics should be the same.

The data in Table 4.3 look at the effect of education on unemployment for different racial groups. By reading across the first four rows, it is clear that for each racial group, unemployment rates tend to decline as education increases. This is consistent with the above argument. However, by reading down each column, it is also clear that at all but two levels of education, whites are less likely to be unemployed than people of color. At the high school graduate level, for example, blacks are twice as likely to be unemployed as whites. However, whereas the unemployment rate of Hispanics is 1.2 times higher than the white rate, the Asian rate is equal to the white rate. This means that differences in education cannot explain all of the racial differences in unemployment.

There are also important racial differences in the kinds of jobs people have. Table 4.4 looks at the distribution of different occupational categories in the United States. The best-paying and most skilled jobs are in the management and professional categories. While 35 percent of whites and 45 percent of Asians are in these two categories, only 26 per-

Table 4.3   Unemployment Rates of Sixteen-Year-Olds and Older in 2004, by Race, Spanish Origin, and Education

Race/ Spanish Origin	Didn't Finish High School (%)	High School Graduate (%)	Some College No Degree (%)	Associate Degree (%)	Bachelor's Degree or More (%)
White	7.5[a]	4.4	3.8	3.3	2.5
Black	15.5	8.7	8.3	5.8	4.3
Asian	5.9	4.5	4.7	4.9	2.9
Hispanic	7.5	5.2	5.0	4.2	3.5
Black/white	2.1[b]	2.0	2.2	1.8	1.7
Asian/white	0.8	1.0	1.2	1.5	1.2
Hispanic/white	1.0	1.2	1.3	1.3	1.4

Source: http://www.bls.gov/cpshome.htm#tables.
Notes: a. E.g., 7.5 percent of whites who didn't complete high school were unemployed.
b. E.g., among those who didn't finish high school, the black unemployment rate was 2.1 times higher than the white rate.

Table 4.4   Employed Persons in 2004, by Occupation, Race, and Spanish Origin

Occupational Category	White (%)	Black (%)	Hispanic (%)	Asian (%)
Management, business	15.3	9.4	7.2	15.1
Professional	20.3	17.0	10.1	30.0
Sales	11.8	9.6	9.2	11.3
Administrative support, office	13.7	16.7	12.1	11.8
Construction/extraction	6.6	3.8	11.9	1.4
Installation/maintenance/ repair	3.8	2.6	4.0	2.6
Production	6.6	7.5	10.6	8.4
Transportation	5.9	9.2	8.7	2.9
Service	15.2	23.8	20.1	16.2
Farming/forestry/fishing	0.8	0.4	2.2	0.4
All occupational categories	100.0	100.0	100.0	100.0

Source: http://www.bls.gov/cpshome.htm#tables.
Note: E.g., 30 percent of Asian workers were in professional occupations but only 10.1 percent of Hispanic workers were in those occupations.

cent of blacks and 17 percent of Hispanics are managers or profession-als. In the lower-paid, lower-skilled service category, in contrast, we find only 15 percent of white workers and 16 percent of Asians, com-pared to 24 percent of black workers and 20 percent of Hispanics. Clearly, Asians and whites are much more likely to have higher-paying jobs than are blacks and Hispanics.

Given these data, it is not unreasonable to expect that incomes for blacks and Hispanics would be substantially lower than incomes for whites and Asians. The first column of Table 4.5 looks at the median in-

Table 4.5   Median Income of Families and Income Ratio in 2003, by Race/Ethnicity and Family Type

Race/Ethnicity	All Families	Married Couples	Male Head	Female Head
White, non-Hispanic	59,937	66,572	41,003	31,639
Black	34,369	52,556	29,788	21,336
Asian	63,251	70,274	54,585	37,243
Hispanic	34,272	40,390	32,120	21,136
Income ratio				
Black/white	0.57	0.79	0.73	0.67
Asian/white	1.06	1.06	1.33	1.18
Hispanic/white	0.57	0.61	0.78	0.67

Source: http://ferret.bls.census.gov/macro/032004/faminc/new01_000.htm.

comes for all families. As predicted, black and Hispanic families earned about 57 percent of the income of white families in 2003. Unfortunately, the black/white ratio has been fairly stable since 1959.

Asian families, in comparison, make slightly *more* than white families. However, it is important to understand the great variation among Asian families. According to the 2000 census, Japanese and Asian Indian families had median incomes of almost $71,000. Hmong and Cambodian families had median incomes of only $32,384 and $35,621, respectively (Watanabe and Wride 2004).

In trying to explain these income differences, many analysts point to differences in family structure. The percentage of female-headed families (i.e., a female adult plus children with no male living regularly in the home) is much higher among blacks than whites. In 2003, for example, 44.8 percent of black families were headed by women compared to 22.3 percent of Hispanic families and 14.3 percent of white families (US Census Bureau 2004a). Female-headed families have much lower incomes than either male-headed families (where there is no woman regularly living in the home) or married-couple families where either one or two of the adults work.

The data in columns two, three, and four in Table 4.5 control for type of family. Reading across the rows, married-couple families in each race/ethnic group earn more than male-headed families who, in turn, earn more than female-headed families. Reading down the columns, the black/white family income gap for married couples declines relative to all families, although it is still substantial. Black married couples earn 79 percent of the income of white married couples, compared to the 57 percent figure for all families. The Asian/white and Hispanic/white income gaps are not heavily impacted by comparing all families with married-couple families. Presumably, differences in the occupational distributions and the unemployment rates contribute to these family income differences. It is also important to note that Asian families earn more than white families in each family type, in part because Asian families tend to have more workers.

These same group differences can also be seen by looking at the incomes of year-round full-time workers in 2003. The data in Table 4.6 show that the white median incomes are higher than the incomes of other racial groups. Among men, Hispanics in 2003 made only 57 percent of the income of whites. Black males made 72 percent of the income of whites. Asians made 99 percent of the income of whites. A similar pattern occurs with racial differences in the incomes of women, though the racial gap for women was smaller than the racial gap for men. Asian women actually had higher incomes in 2003 than white women.

Table 4.6 **Median Income and Income Ratio of Year-Round Full-Time Workers Age Fifteen and Older in 2003, by Race/Ethnicity and Sex**

Race/Ethnicity	Sex		
	Male	Female	Female/Male Income Ratio[a]
White, nonhispanic	$46,294	$32,192	0.70
Black	33,429	27,622	0.83
Asian	46,220	34,584	0.75
Hispanic	26,414	23,062	0.87
All workers	41,503	31,653	0.76
Income ratio			
Black/white	0.72	0.86	—
Asian/white	0.99	1.07	—
Hispanic/white	0.57	0.72	—

Source: http://ferret.bls.census.gov/macro/032004/perinc/toc.htm.
Notes: a. Female income divided by male income. For example, among white non-Hispanic workers, women earn 70 percent of the income that a male earns.

Table 4.6 also shows the gender gaps in income within a given race. The female-to-male income gap was highest among whites and Asians (0.70 and 0.75, respectively) and was lowest among blacks and Hispanics (0.83 and 0.87, respectively). In other words, among non-Hispanic whites, women earn only 70 cents for each dollar a man earns. Hispanic women, on the other hand, earn 87 cents for each dollar that a Hispanic male earns. We will discuss gender differences in more detail in the following chapter.

We can also look at the trends in racial income gaps over time, as illustrated in Table 4.7. Looking at the income ratio for blacks relative to whites, we can see that the income gap between black and white men has closed slightly from 1967 to 2003. In contrast, the income gap between Hispanic and white men has actually increased between the early 1970s and 2003. The gap between Asian and white men seems to have disappeared. Looking at women, the black/white income gap declined substantially between 1967 and 1980 but then began to increase once again. The Hispanic/white gap for women, like that for men, has grown since the early 1970s. Asian women, however, continue to earn slightly more than white women. The income trends for black and Hispanic women are not encouraging.

There are also differences in poverty rates. In 2003, 8.2 percent of non-Hispanic whites were poor compared with 24.4 percent of blacks,

Table 4.7   Median Income and Income Ratio of Year-Round Full-Time Workers, 1967–2003, by Race/Ethnicity and Gender

Year	White Median Income	Black Median Income	Hispanic Median Income	Asian Median Income	Black/ White Income Ratio	Hispanic/ White Income Ratio	Asian/ White Income Ratio
Males							
1967	$7,396	$4,777	—	—	0.65	—	—
1970	9,223	6,368	$8,885[a]	—	0.69	0.73[a]	—
1980	19,157	13,547	13,558	—	0.71	0.71	—
1990	28,881	21,114	19,136	$26,765	0.73	0.66	0.93
2000	38,637	30,101	23,778	40,556	0.78	0.62	1.05
2003	46,294	33,429	26,414	46,220	0.72	0.57	0.99
Females							
1967	$4,279	$3,194	—	—	0.75	—	—
1970	5,412	4,447	$5,925[a]	—	0.82	0.84[a]	—
1980	11,277	10,672	9,679	—	0.95	0.86	—
1990	20,048	18,040	15,672	$21,324	0.90	0.78	1.06
2000	28,243	25,089	20,659	30,475	0.89	0.73	1.08
2003	32,192	27,622	23,062	34,584	0.86	0.72	1.07

Source: Current Population Survey, Annual Demographic Supplements, http://www.census.gov/hhes/income/historic/p38d.html.
Note: a. Based on 1974 data.

8.2 percent of Hispanics, and 11.8 percent of Asians. In spite of these important differences in poverty rates, there were more poor non-Hispanic whites (15.9 million) than poor blacks (8.8 million) or poor Hispanics (9.1 million). The reason for this apparent contradiction is that non-Hispanic whites make up such a large percentage of the total population. Even though their rate of poverty is relatively low, the absolute number of poor non-Hispanic whites is very large (www.census.gov/hhes/www/poverty/poverty04/table3.pdf).

Racial differences in wealth are even more unequal than the differences in income. Table 4.8 shows that in 2002, non-Hispanic white households had a median net worth of $88,651, compared to only $7,932 for Hispanics and $5,988 for blacks. This means that Hispanics' net worth is only 8.9 percent that of non-Hispanic whites and that blacks' net worth is only 6.8 percent that of non-Hispanic whites. Between 1996 and 2002, the value of non-Hispanic white and Hispanic net worth increased by 17.4 percent and 14.0 percent, respectively. Black net worth declined by 16.1 percent during this time.

There are also major differences in educational attainment by race and ethnicity. Table 4.9 shows that almost half of Asians had a bachelor's degree or higher in 2003. Only 30.1 percent of non-Hispanic whites, 17.3 percent of blacks, and 11.4 percent of Hispanics had bachelor's de-

Table 4.8   Median Net Worth (in 2003 dollars) of Households in 1996 and 2002, by Race and Ethnicity

	1996		2002		
Race/Ethnicity	Net Worth	Percentage of Non-Hispanic White	Net Worth	Percentage of Non-Hispanic White	Percentage Change 1996–2002
Non-Hispanic white	$75,482	—	$88,651	—	+17.4
Non-Hispanic black	7,135	9.5%	5,988	6.8%	−16.1
Hispanic	6,961	9.2	7,932	8.9	+14.0
All households	53,160	—	59,706	—	+12.3

Source: Kochhar 2004.

grees or higher. At the other end of the spectrum, 43.0 percent of Hispanics did not finish high school, compared with 20.0 percent of blacks, 12.4 percent of Asians, and 10.6 percent of non-Hispanic whites.

Once again, there are great variations among different Asian groups. According to the 2000 census, 63.9 percent of Asian Indians had bachelor's degrees or higher. However, less than 10 percent of Cambodians, Hmongs, and Laotians had bachelor's degrees or higher (Watanabe and Wride 2004).

It is also important to look at trends in educational attainment. By reading down the columns in Table 4.10, it is clear that the percentage of each race/ethnic group that has completed high school and college is

Table 4.9   Educational Attainment of US Population Twenty-five Years Old and Older by Race/Ethnic Group in 2003

Highest Level of Education Reached	Non-Hispanic Whites	Black	Hispanic	Asian
Eighth grade or less	3.6%	6.4%	26.1%	7.5%
Some high school	7.0	13.6	16.9	4.9
High school graduate	32.9	35.2	27.4	20.3
Some college	17.6	19.9	13.0	11.0
AA degree	8.8	7.5	5.2	6.6
BA degree	19.7	12.2	8.3	31.2
MA degree	7.4	4.0	2.1	12.5
PhD degree	1.3	0.5	0.4	3.1
First professional degree	1.7	0.6	0.6	3.0
Total	100.0	100.0	100.0	100.0

Source: Chronicle of Higher Education 2004.

Table 4.10 Percentage of Persons Twenty-five Years and Older Who Completed High School and College, by Race/Ethnicity

Year	Completed Four Years of High School or More					Completed Four Years of College or More				
	White	Black	Hispanic	W/B[a]	W/H[a]	White	Black	Hispanic	W/B[a]	W/H[a]
1940	26.1	7.7	—	3.39	—	4.9	1.3	—	3.77	—
1950	36.4	13.7	—	2.66	—	6.6	2.2	—	3.00	—
1960	43.2	21.7	—	1.99	—	8.1	3.5	—	2.31	—
1970	57.4	36.1	—	1.59	—	11.6	6.1	—	1.90	—
1980[b]	71.9	51.4	44.5	1.40	1.62	18.4	7.9	7.6	2.33	2.42
1990	81.4	66.2	50.8	1.23	1.60	23.1	11.3	9.2	2.04	2.51
2000	88.4	78.9	57.0	1.12	1.55	28.1	16.6	10.6	1.69	2.65
2003	89.4	80.0	57.0	1.12	1.57	30.0	17.3	11.4	1.73	2.63

Source: Harvey and Anderson 2005; National Center for Education Statistics, http://nces.ed.gov/programs/digest/d02/tables/dt008.asp.

Notes: E.g., in 2000, 88.4 percent of whites, 78.9 percent of blacks, and 57.0 percent of Hispanics had completed four years of high school or more.

a. White rate divided by black (or Hispanic) rate. In 2000, for example, whites were 2.65 times more likely than Hispanics to complete four years of college or more.

b. Since 1980, data refer to non-Hispanic whites and non-Hispanic blacks.

increasing. The black/white gap in high school graduation rates has almost disappeared. In 1940, whites were more than three times more likely than blacks to graduate from high school. By 2003, whites were only slightly more likely than blacks to be high school graduates. The Hispanic/white gap increased slightly since 1980. The Department of Education doesn't track these data for Asians.

The black/white gap in college graduation rates has also declined sharply, but it is still substantial. In 2003, whites were 1.73 times more likely to graduate from college than blacks. Whites are more than 2.5 times more likely to graduate from college than Hispanics, and the gap has grown larger since 1980. Aside from moving toward parity in the black/white high school graduation rates, educational inequality is still a serious problem.

Some of the racial gap in income can probably be explained by differences in education. What would happen if we control for education and then look at racial differences in income? These data are presented in Table 4.11. Reading down the columns, we see that for each race/ethnic group, a higher level of education results in higher incomes. This is true for both males and females.

Reading across the rows, it is possible to compare each race/ethnic group at the same level of education. Among males, non-Hispanic whites have higher incomes than men of color at the same educational level in all cases but one. For men with bachelor's degrees but no advanced degrees, for example, blacks made 76 percent the income of whites, Asians made 91 percent the income of whites, and Hispanics made 75 percent the income of whites. Asian males come the closest to having income parity with white males.

The data for women are similar. After controlling for education, white women had higher incomes than women of color in all cases but two. Once again, Asian women are the closest to having income parity with white women and in two cases even exceed the income of white women. It is also important to note that after controlling for education, women in each race/ethnic group earn lower incomes than comparable men. We will return to this issue in the next chapter.

These data show continuing inequalities between whites and non-Asian people of color. In spite of some dramatic closing of the gap in educational attainment and some minor improvements in the income gap, economic inequality remains substantial. Asians have exceeded whites in educational attainment and have come the closest to having parity with whites in terms of income. There is still a lot of work to be done.

Table 4.11 Median Income of Year-Round Full-Time Workers in 2003, by Race/Ethnicity, Sex, and Education

Education/Sex	Median Income by Race/Ethnicity				Income Ratio Comparison with Whites		
	White Non-Hispanic	Black	Asian	Hispanic	Black/White NH[a]	Asian/White NH	Hispanic/White NH
Males							
Grades 9–12	$30,933	$21,995	$28,329	$24,102	0.71	0.92	0.78
HS graduate	39,207	30,830	30,346	29,376	0.79	0.77	0.75
Some college	45,513	35,958	35,959	37,320	0.79	0.79	0.82
AA degree	46,384	40,562	41,413	38,488	0.87	0.89	0.83
BA degree +	68,545	50,738	65,635	50,871	0.74	0.96	0.74
BA only	61,133	46,749	55,380	45,879	0.76	0.91	0.75
MA	75,262	60,870	76,757	61,524	0.81	1.02	0.82
Professional	100,000	—	83,422	—	—	0.83	—
PhD	93,766	—	85,221	—	—	0.91	—
Females							
Grades 9–12	20,001	19,371	—	16,634	0.97	—	0.83
HS graduate	27,668	24,718	23,569	23,349	0.89	0.85	0.84
Some college	31,756	28,873	29,197	27,289	0.91	0.92	0.86
AA degree	35,229	30,202	31,983	31,220	0.86	0.91	0.89
BA degree +	46,637	41,729	50,416	41,679	0.89	1.08	0.89
BA only	42,781	39,850	46,585	38,813	0.93	1.09	0.91
MA	51,554	48,862	51,033	51,164	0.95	0.99	0.99
Professional	69,449	—	—	—	—	—	—
PhD	70,381	—	—	—	—	—	—

Source: US Census Bureau, http://www.ferret.bls.census.gov/macro/032004/perinc/new01_040.htm.
Note: a. White NH: white non-Hispanic.

▣ Prejudice and Ideology

There has been a long tradition in the fields of sociology and social psychology of studying racial prejudice. Until very recently, most of the studies addressed the issue of white prejudice toward blacks. Since this is part of a single chapter in a small book, I will focus on the black-white issue.

Most social scientists recognize that prejudice today is not the same as it was 100 years ago or even 50 years ago. The **traditional prejudice** of the past focused on beliefs of black biological inferiority and the support of formal racial separation. Typical measures of traditional prejudice might have asked respondents to agree or disagree with the following statements:

"There should be laws against racial intermarriage."
"Blacks and whites should not attend the same schools."
"As a race, blacks are less intelligent than whites."

Most of us would acknowledge that agreeing with these statements would indicate that the respondent was prejudiced.

Most studies have shown that whereas a majority of whites would have agreed with these statements 100 years ago, only a small percentage still agreed with them after the 1960s. There are several different interpretations of these findings. On the one hand, it's possible that traditional prejudice among the white population has declined dramatically. On the other hand, it's possible that whites still believe these things but won't say so to an interviewer because it is no longer the socially desirable response. Although social desirability is an important factor, I think that most whites in the twenty-first century see traditional prejudice as outdated and abhorrent.

However, this doesn't let whites off the hook, because many whites still hold other negative and/or distorted attitudes toward blacks. Consider these results from a 2003 national survey of adults eighteen years of age and older by the American Association of Retired People (2004). In response to a question about contemporary black civil rights groups, 43 percent of non-Hispanic whites felt that they were asking for too much, 14 percent said they were asking for too little, and 40 percent said they were asking for the right amount. Sixty-one percent of non-Hispanic whites believed that blacks and whites had equal job opportunities, and 78 percent believed that no new civil rights laws were needed to protect blacks.

Increasingly, social scientists argue that since the 1970s, a new form of antiblack prejudice has replaced the traditional form. This **new prejudice** (often referred to as "racism") goes under a variety of different labels—symbolic racism, modern racism, aversive racism, color-blind racism, laissez-faire racism, and social dominance orientation (Jones 1997; Bonilla-Silva 2003). Although there are some differences between them, the discussions of the new prejudice have certain factors in common:

1. A rejection of traditional prejudice and seeing oneself as non-prejudiced
2. A rejection of legal discrimination and the belief that racial discrimination is a thing of the past
3. A negative attitude toward blacks based on fear and resentment, which is usually expressed indirectly
4. An ambivalence between a person's egalitarian ideals and negative feelings toward blacks
5. A belief that black culture causes black inequality

Measures of the new prejudice might include the following statements:

"Blacks are getting too demanding in their push for equal rights."
"Discrimination against blacks is no longer a problem."
"Over the past few years, the government and the news media have shown more respect to blacks than they deserve."
"Blacks would be more successful if they worked harder."

Agreement with these questions would indicate prejudice, and disagreement would indicate nonprejudice. Using these questions, a substantial proportion of whites would score high on measures of the new prejudice. Proponents of the new prejudice viewpoint argue that this type of prejudice is neither better nor worse than traditional prejudice; it's just different.

Some social scientists, especially conservatives, reject the idea that there is a new prejudice. They see the new prejudice concept as a misguided liberal attempt to equate conservative ideology with antiblack attitudes (Roth 1994). Traditional prejudice is the only valid type of prejudice, according to conservatives, and that has diminished.

Regardless of the type of prejudice we are discussing, most social scientists would agree that prejudice involves a set of negative attitudes held by individuals. People learn these attitudes from their families, their peer groups, the media, the schools, and other social institutions. Social psychologists have also argued that racial prejudice serves certain personality functions among white individuals. Given this approach, these negative attitudes would predispose people to discriminate against and/or to reject policies that might benefit the black community. Because the prejudiced attitudes are an important cause of the discriminatory behavior and policies, according to this view, if one could change the individual attitudes, it would be easier to change social policies.

But negative attitudes are also part of a racial ideology that is used to explain and justify racial oppression. Eduardo Bonilla-Silva (2003, 2), for example, argues that color-blind racism

> explains contemporary racial inequality as the outcome of nonracial dynamics. Whereas Jim Crow racism [in the South before the 1960s] explained blacks' social standing as the result of their biological and moral inferiority, color-blind racism avoids such facile arguments. Instead, whites rationalize minorities' contemporary status as the product of market dynamics, naturally occurring phenomena, and blacks' imputed cultural limitations. For instance, whites can attribute Latinos' high poverty rate to a relaxed work ethic ("the Hispanics are *mañana, mañana, mañana*—tomorrow, tomorrow, tomorrow") or residential segregation as the result of natural tendencies among groups ("Do a cat and a dog mix?").

In other words, Bonilla-Silva argues that color-blind racial ideology is not the *cause* of racial inequality but the *result* or justification of inequality.

Discrimination

In spite of what many white Americans might think, discrimination is not a thing of the past. Previously, I defined discrimination as actions that deny equal treatment to persons believed to be members of some racial category or group. As I have shown in the previous section, most white Americans no longer see racial discrimination as a serious problem. They typically point to the demise of legal segregation in the South and the passage of numerous civil rights legislations at the federal, state, and local levels.

Although it is certainly true that substantial progress has been made in the past half-century, racial discrimination is still alive and well. At the individual level, discrimination refers to the behavior of members of one racial group/category that is intended to have a differential and/or harmful effect on members of another racial group/category. These discriminatory actions can range from racial slurs and graffiti, to not being hired or being unfairly fired, to not being able to rent an apartment or secure a home mortgage, to being physically assaulted. It is difficult to quantify these individual-level actions.

Studies of college campuses, for example, suggest that as many as one in four students of color experiences an ethnoviolent act on campus in a given academic year (Ehrlich 1999). **Ethnoviolence** refers to *acts motivated by prejudice intending to do physical or psychological harm because of their group membership.* Most ethnoviolent acts involve name-calling and graffiti, though a small percentage involve physical violence. With more than 4 million students of color in the nation's colleges and universities, as many as 1 million college students may be victimized on campus in any given year. The Southern Poverty Law Center (2004) puts this estimate at more than 500,000 annually.

These actions are almost certainly more common in public spaces off campus (Feagin 1991). According to Federal Bureau of Investigation (2004) statistics, 3,844 race-based hate crimes were reported to the police in 2003. Of this number, 2,548 were antiblack, 830 were antiwhite, 231 were anti-Asian, and 76 were anti–Native American. In addition, 1,026 hate crimes were based on ethnicity or national origin, with 426 being anti-Hispanic. Finally, 1,343 hate crimes were based on religion—927 against Jews and 149 against Muslims.

Most social scientists would agree that these figures represent a small fraction of the hate crimes committed that year, since most victims don't report them to the police and local police are inconsistent about reporting to the FBI. According to the Council on American-Islamic Relations, for example, there were 926 instances of anti-Muslim harassment and discrimination in 2003, a sharp increase over the previous year (Langfitt 2004). The National Association of Asian Pacific American Legal Consortium documented 275 anti-Asian bias crimes in 2002, 40 percent of which were against South Asian Muslims and Sikhs (Haniffa 2004).

Similarly, it is impossible to determine the true number of cases of employment discrimination experienced by people of color. In the four-year period of 2000–2003, more than 116,000 complaints alleging race discrimination in employment were filed with the federal Equal Employment Opportunity Commission (2004a). Hundreds of thousands more were filed at the state level. The overwhelming majority of these cases were filed by persons of color.

Proving that you have been victimized by employment discrimination is extremely difficult, either at the EEOC level or in a court of law. My own research suggests that the EEOC rules in favor of the complainant in race discrimination cases in only 12 percent of the cases (Pincus 2003). Of the aforementioned 116,0000 complaints filed in 2000–2003, the EEOC documented only 14,000 cases of employment discrimination.

Two recent studies, however, suggest that employment discrimination is much more widespread. Devah Pager (2003) sent out fictitious resumes to Milwaukee, Wisconsin–area employers. Half were from blacks and half from whites. Within each racial group, half had criminal records and the other half did not. Other than race and criminal record, the resumes were comparable. The main variable was whether the fictitious applicant would be invited for an interview. To no one's surprise, whites with no criminal record were most likely to be called in, and blacks with a record were least likely. The most shocking finding, however, was that whereas 17 percent of the whites with criminal records were called for an interview, only 14 percent of the blacks without a record were called for an interview. In this study, race was a more important factor than having a criminal record.

In a second study, Sendhil Mullainathan and Marianne Bertrand sent 5,000 resumes in response to employment ads in Boston and Chicago (Glenn 2003; Associated Press 2003). Each employer received four resumes. Half of the resumes showed weak employment histories and job skills, and the other half showed strong employment histories and skills. In addition, half of the resumes had stereotypical black names like Lakisha and Jamal, while the other half had more white-sounding names like Emily or John. Each resume had a phone number with a voice-mail message by someone of the appropriate race and gender.

Once again, race was a factor in who got a call-back. The white-sounding names got a callback once for every ten resumes sent out; the black-sounding names got one callback for every fifteen resumes. The Kristens and Carries got callbacks 13 percent of the time, whereas the Keishas and Tamikas got callbacks less than 4 percent of the time.

Having a strong resume helped whites more than blacks. Among the white-sounding names, having a strong resume increased the likelihood of getting a callback by 30 percent compared to the weak resumes. For the black-sounding names, having a strong resume increased the callback likelihood by only 9 percent.

These two recent studies are consistent with the findings of older studies that actually sent matched pairs of students (white and black or white and Hispanic) to apply in person for a job. In these studies, discrimination occurred about 20 percent of the time (Bendick, Jackson, and Reinoso 1994). All these data clearly show that employment discrimination is still an issue.

Discrimination is not just practiced at the individual level by small employers and managers. Institutional discrimination remains in place as well. Following are some examples of out-of-court settlements in 2004 and early 2005 involving allegations of institutional race discrimination. Typically, the employer agrees to pay a fine and change its procedures without admitting any wrongdoing.

- Sodexho, a multinational food conglomerate, paid $80 million to 3,400 black middle-level managers who charged that they were passed over for promotion because of their race. Although 12 percent of Sodexho's managers are black, only 2 percent of the upper-level managers are black (Shin 2005).
- The New York City Police Department reached a $26.8 million out-of-court settlement in a class-action lawsuit filed by black and Hispanic officers. In 1999 the officers had charged the department with creating hostile work environments, retaliating against officers who complained, and operating a discriminatory disciplinary system. Some 12,000 black and Hispanic officers could receive between $3,500 and $400,000 each. This is an example of intentional institutional discrimination.
- Clothing retailer Abercrombie and Fitch paid $50 million in response to charges that Latino and Asian workers either were not hired at all or were relegated to working behind the scenes in store stockrooms (Cole 2004). White, blond-haired, attractive salespeople were preferred to maintain a "preppy" corporate image. According to the settlement, the company agreed to hire a vice president for diversity and to submit to monitoring for a period of years. The plaintiffs received between $5,000 and $39,000 each.
- Global Building Services, which had a contract from the retailer Target to clean Target stores in five states, paid $1.9 million for not paying overtime to immigrants who worked as janitors (*New York Times* News Service 2004). According to the charges, GBS paid the workers in cash and failed to withhold payroll taxes and workers' compensation. Janitors were forced to work seven days a week.
- Wal-Mart paid an $11 million fine for working with contractors who employed illegal immigrants in more than 1,000 of its stores

throughout the country. A spokesperson said that although executives and middle-level managers didn't know what was going on, "We acknowledge we should have had better safeguards in place" (Wire Services 2005, C14).

• R. R. Donnelley and Sons, a large printing corporation, paid $15 million for discriminating against black workers in a now-closed plant (*Diversity News* 2004d). White coworkers also used nooses and Ku Klux Klan uniforms to intimidate black workers.

Not all the race discrimination cases involved employer-employee relations. The Cracker Barrel Restaurant chain was charged with segregated seating patterns and making blacks wait for excessively long times (DiversityInc Staff and Associated Press 2004). Cracker Barrel did not have to pay a fine but agreed to diversity training and to be monitored by a firm that would send in "undercover" customers.

Finally, Continental Airlines settled a racial profiling case brought by the Department of Transportation (*Diversity News* 2004e). Continental was charged with discriminatory practices against Arab and Muslim passengers after September 11. The company paid no fine but agreed to diversity training for pilots and flight attendants. Similar settlements had been worked out with United and American Airlines.

Readers may wonder why there is so much talk about fines in these race discrimination cases and no talk of jail sentences. That's because employment discrimination is a violation of civil law, not criminal law. An employer can't go to jail for refusing to hire or promote someone because of his or her race.

An example of structural discrimination occurred in the Baltimore City Fire Department (BCFD). In winter 2004, the BCFD admitted an all-white class to its fire academy. This was the first time since the department integrated in 1953 that the class was composed only of whites. Although the population of Baltimore is 65 percent black, the BCFD is only 25 percent black (Fields 2004a, 2004b). As an explanation, officials said that relatively few blacks took the test, even fewer passed the test, and most of those who did were disqualified because of criminal records and failed drug tests.

Several factors about the test, however, favored white applicants. First, the test was not offered frequently or at regular intervals; the department's policy is to offer the test every eighteen months to three years. To make matters worse, the test was not advertised due to the lack of an advertising budget, so news of the test was based largely on word of mouth. Finally, the content of the test was based on prior firefighting knowledge rather than general aptitude. Hence, the entire structure of the test favored whites since they were more likely to belong to the in-group and more likely to have participated in rural and suburban volunteer firefighting companies. This could also explain why in spite of a BCFD policy of hiring Baltimore residents, only five out of the thirty recruits lived in the city. This is an example of structural discrimination because even if there was no intention to discriminate against blacks, the test had that effect.

A few days after the city's main newspaper ran a front-page story about the all-white class, embarrassed city officials announced immediate changes. The test will be offered monthly and will be advertised widely throughout Baltimore. This will increase the number of blacks who take the test. The BCFD appointed a recruitment committee that would oversee diversity efforts. Applicants who had completed a certified emergency medical technician program could be admitted without taking the exam. Finally, BCFD officials would see whether a different kind of exam would be more appropriate.

*   *   *

Although many readers might not believe that racial discrimination and prejudice still occur in the twenty-first century, the empirical data show that they do. Civil rights laws have not eliminated discrimination, although they have made it easier to prosecute. In sum, people of color still lack the equality of opportunity in the United States.

5

Gender

THE CONFLICTS BETWEEN MEN AND WOMEN ARE DIFFERENT FROM
the class and race conflicts that we discussed in previous chapters. People of different classes and races often live very separate lives and often
don't have direct interactions with one another. If they do have contact,
it is often in very impersonal ways. Men and women, on the other hand,
live together in families and have intimate contacts with one another.
Most children know both male and female peers as well as adult relatives. In spite of this more personal contact, gender conflict has some of
the same structural issues as do race and class conflict.

▣ Terminology

Although people, including social scientists, often use the terms *sex* and
gender interchangeably, they are really quite different. **Sex** *refers to the
physical and biological differences between the categories of male and
female.* This includes hormones, reproductive apparatus, body shape,
and other physiological characteristics. **Gender** *refers to the behavior
that is culturally defined as appropriate and inappropriate for males
and females.* Gender, therefore, is totally socially constructed whereas
sex has *some* basis in physical reality.

Although this distinction seems simple enough, the reality is considerably more complex. The ability to bear and breastfeed a child, for
example, is clearly related to sex differences. Women can do it and men
can't. But what of the fact that in most societies, including our own,
women tend to do most of the childcare work, both at home and in the

77

paid labor force? Most social scientists would argue that this has to do with gender, not with sex. Physically, men can care for children and feed them out of bottles, either with formula or with expressed breast milk. Culturally, however, this is often defined as women's work.

Of course, sex (that is, physiological) differences are not always clearly defined. A small minority of the population is **intersexed** *in that they have physical attributes of both males and females.* At birth, it is sometimes difficult to tell if a baby is male or female because the genitalia are ambiguous. For years, pediatricians have suggested that surgery be performed on babies so that they can be assigned to one sex or the other. Is someone with both a penis and a vagina a male, or female? What happens when hormones may be inconsistent with chromosomes? In our society, we think we have to know which of the two sexes this individual *really* belongs to. The character of Pat on *Saturday Night Live* is continually frustrating to audiences because of her/his sexual ambiguity.

Anne Fausto-Sterling (1993, 2000) has done some fascinating writing on this topic. In a well-known 1993 article, she argued that there are really five sexes, not just two. "True hermaphrodites," who have one testis and one ovary, she called *herms.* Female pseudohermaphrodites, who have ovaries and some aspect of male genitalia but who do not have testis, are called *ferms.* Male pseudohermaphrodites, who have testis and some aspects of female genitalia but who don't have ovaries, she calls *merms.* Rather than trying to force the herms, ferms, and merms into the categories of male and female, Fausto-Sterling argues that there are five different sexes. In a subsequent article, Fausto-Sterling (2000) rejects her own five-sexes argument and says that sex should not be seen as a simple continuum: "Sex and gender are best conceptualized as points in a multidimensional space. . . . The medical and scientific communities have yet to adopt a language that is capable of describing such diversity" (107).

Transgendered people, for example, *feel that their gender identity doesn't match their physiological body.* These are physiological men who feel female, or physiological women who feel like men. One of my female students, who identifies as a lesbian, has a female partner who is transgendered. Although the partner always dressed in male-like clothing, at one point the partner decided to live as a male by taking a male name and insisting that everyone use the masculine pronoun to refer to her/him. After a few months, the partner returned to the female name. Eventually, she began the complex transition process that will end in his becoming a female-to-male transsexual.

When transgendered people take hormones, begin to live as the opposite sex, and have sex-change operations, they are **transsexuals**. This raises some really mind-blowing questions. Is a male-to-female transsexual a woman or a man? Should one refer to a transsexual as a he or as a she? Which bathroom should s/he use? If a female-to-male transsexual has sexual relations with the man s/he used to be married to, is this a heterosexual, or homosexual, relationship? As I wrote earlier, the male/female dichotomy is not as simple as it seems (Boylan 2003).

Gender is even more fluid than sex. First, gender varies from culture to culture. Men, for example, tend to be much more emotionally and physically expressive in many Hispanic cultures than in the United States. Gender also varies in a single culture over time; for instance, men in our country are much more involved with their children now than they were fifty years ago. Gender also varies within a culture: working mothers have always been more prevalent among working-class and black women than among middle-class and white women. Gender is also situational. Men hugging each other on the athletic field is not viewed in the same light as that action on a street corner. As Michael Kimmel writes,

> [Our gender] identities are a fluid assemblage of the meanings and behaviors that we construct from the values, images, and prescriptions we find in the world around us. Our gender identities are both voluntary—we choose to become who we are—and coerced—we are pressured, forced, sanctioned, and often physically beaten into submission to some rules. We neither make up the rules as we go along nor do we glide perfectly and effortlessly into preassigned roles. (2004, 194)

Understanding gender relations involves more than just culture. It also involves power and hierarchy. Most social scientists who write about gender would define **patriarchy** *as a hierarchical system that promotes male supremacy.* This refers to a set of institutions that are organized in a way that benefits the majority of men over the majority of women in the economy, the political system, the family, and so on. Of course, not all men benefit from patriarchy in the same way, and not all women are hurt in the same way. In fact, a small group of wealthy white men are at the top of the patriarchy, and they have power over all women and most men.

Many men reject the concept of patriarchy by saying that they don't *feel* powerful. Working-class and poor men have little power due to their *class* position, and men of color have little power due to their *race.*

However, most of these men, along with white middle-class men, do exert power over women in their families, in their workplaces, and in their communities. The concept of patriarchy is not an all-or-nothing concept. Different men benefit in different ways.

Finally, we come to the concept of sexism. Like the concept of racism, discussed in the previous chapter, the term *sexism* has been used in a variety of ways since the 1960s. Some see sexism as an ideological support for patriarchy. This refers to a set of cultural beliefs and personal attitudes that support male control of major social institutions. According to this view, believing that men should be the head of the house or that women should not supervise men on the job would be considered sexist. Later in the chapter, I will discuss the way social psychologists measure sexist beliefs.

Though others agree, they would extend the term to include both attitudes and behaviors that hurt women. According to this argument, those who refuse to hire women as managers or those who commit violence against women are exhibiting sexist behavior. It's not just the attitudes that are the problem, it's also the behavior.

Still others use *sexism* synonymously with patriarchy to describe a gender-based system of oppression that would include ideology and attitudes as well as behavior and institutional organization. In this case laws and religious practices that discriminate against women would be considered sexist. The important point here is that all the writers agree that there is a system that oppresses women and that part of that system consists of ideology and attitudes. The disagreement is over what labels to use.

In this book, I will use the more inclusive use of **sexism** as *a system of oppression based on gender.* This would include prejudice and discrimination toward women as well as ideologies and policies that keep women as second-class citizens. Since only women are oppressed because of their gender, only men and male-dominated institutions can be sexist according to this definition. Women, of course, can be prejudiced toward men and, in some limited cases, have the power to discriminate against men. As much as we may dislike these activities, they are not sexist because they are not part of an oppressive system. More than two decades ago, Marilyn Frye (1983) argued that though men can (and should) be unhappy because they can't express their feelings, this is not the same as being oppressed.

Finally, we come to the concept of *feminism,* which is often associated with what has come to be known as the women's liberation movement. Although most young women believe in things like equal pay for equal work, the need for more women in traditionally male jobs, and the need for men and women to share in childcare and housework, they would not describe themselves as feminist. What does feminism mean and why is it so threatening?

More than twenty years ago, bell hooks wrote, "A central problem within feminist discourse has been our inability to either arrive at a consensus of opinion about what feminism is or accept definition(s) that could serve as points of unification" (hooks 2000, 238). This statement is still true today since there are a variety of different types of feminism. Price and Sokoloff (2004), for example, describe five approaches to feminism:

- *Liberal feminism*, the most mainstream of the perspectives, stresses the importance of equality of women with men within the *existing* political and economic structures in society. From this perspective, the most common cause of gender inequality is identified as cultural attitudes with regard to gender role socialization. . . .
- *Radical feminism* identifies male dominance and control as the cause of gender inequality and argues that these must be eliminated from all social institutions. Men's control of women's sexuality and the norm of heterosexuality are identified as the core of women's oppression. . . .
- *Marxist feminism* views women's oppression as a function of class relations in a capitalist society. . . . Women are twice burdened in this analysis; they are oppressed economically in low-wage jobs in the labor market and they are oppressed by their unpaid family responsibilities centered around reproductive labor (childbearing, childcare and housework). . . .
- *Socialist feminists* combine the Marxist and radical feminist perspectives and identify as the causes of gender inequality and women's oppression both patriarchy and capitalism in public as well as private spheres of life. . . .
- *Women of color feminists* . . . introduce the concept of "intersectionalities" to understand the interlocking *sites* of oppression; they examine how the categories of race, class, gender and sexuality in intersecting systems of domination rely on each other to function. (2–3; also see Lorber 1998)

These diverse viewpoints can be frustrating for those who want a short answer to the apparently simple question, What do feminists believe? Fortunately, Margaret Anderson (2003, 9) tries to identify some of the issues that are common to all forms of feminism:

> Feminism begins with the premise that women's and men's positions
> in society are the result of social, not natural or biological factors. . . .
> Feminists generally see social institutions and social attitudes as the
> basis for women's position in society. Because in sexist societies these
> institutions have created structured inequities between women and
> men, feminists believe in transforming institutions to generate liberat-
> ing social changes on behalf of women; thus, feminism takes women's
> interests and perspectives seriously, believing that women are not in-
> ferior to men. Feminism is a way of both thinking and acting; in fact,
> the union of action and thought is central to feminist programs for so-
> cial change. Although feminists do not believe that women should be
> like men, they do believe that women's experiences, concerns and
> ideas are as valuable as those of men and should be treated with equal
> seriousness and respect. As a result, feminism makes women's inter-
> ests central in movement for social change.

This view of feminism is quite different from the popular stereotype of
bra-burning, man-hating lesbians that many people wrongly associate
with feminism. Although many lesbians are feminists, the overwhelming number of feminists are not lesbians. Although some feminists hate
men, most do not. The bra-burning stereotype stems from a 1968 protest
of the Miss America pageant in Atlantic City, New Jersey. Some of the
200 protesters threw bras and high heels into a "freedom trash can" to
oppose the sexual objectification of women; they never burned them
(Albert and Albert 1984).

So, what is the definition of feminism? My own inclination is to go
with Anderson's general comments cited above and to read about the
different types of feminism in Ollenburger and Moore (1998), Lorber
(1998), or Renzetti and Curran (1999). For those who absolutely need a
formal definition, here's a short, snappy one provided by bell hooks
(2000, 240): **feminism** is *"a movement to end sexist oppression."*

▓ Descriptive Statistics

In discussing gender in the United States, it is important to understand
that the majority of women work in the paid labor force. I use the phrase
"work in the paid labor force" to underscore the importance of work
that women perform in the home as housewives and mothers; they just
don't get paid for it.

According to the most recent data in Table 5.1, 60.6 percent of
women twenty years old and older worked in the paid labor force in

Table 5.1 Labor Force Participation Rates of Persons Twenty Years
Old and Older, 1948–2003, by Race/Ethnicity and Sex

	Total Population		Whites		Blacks		Hispanics	
	Male	Female	Male	Female	Male	Female	Male	Female
1948	88.6	31.8	—	—	—	—	—	—
1960	86.6	37.6	—	—	—	—	—	—
1970	82.6	43.3	82.8	42.2	78.4[a]	51.6[a]	85.9[a]	41.3[a]
1980	79.4	51.3	79.8	50.6	75.1	55.6	84.9	48.5
1990	78.2	58.0	78.5	57.6	75.0	60.6	84.7	54.8
2000	76.7	60.6	77.1	59.9	72.8	65.4	85.3	59.3
2003	75.9	60.6	76.3	59.9	71.5	64.6	84.1	58.1

Source: US Department of Labor, http://stats.bls.gov/cps/cpsatabs.htm.
Note: a. 1973 data.

2003, compared to 75.9 percent of the men. More than three-quarters of
married women with children ages six to seventeen work. Even 58 percent of married women with children three years old or younger work
in the paid labor force. The stay-at-home housewife/mom is becoming
a thing of the past.

There has been a sea change in the labor force participation rates of
women over the past sixty years. The data in Table 5.1 show that in 1948,
only 31.8 percent of all women worked in the paid labor force. In other
words, the labor force participation rate for women has almost doubled
since 1948. This increasing labor force participation rate applies to single women, married women, and women with young children.

In comparison, men are less likely to be in the labor force now
(75.9 percent) than in 1948. Although men have always been more
likely than women to work in the paid labor force, the gap has been
steadily declining.

These same trends are true when whites, blacks, and Hispanics are
compared. The labor force participation rates of white, black, and Hispanic women have increased dramatically since 1970, when data gath-
ering for these groups began. More than 70 percent of black married
women with children under three are in the paid labor force. The rates
for white and black men have declined. Hispanic men, who have the
highest participation rates of any of the race/gender groups, have been
employed at a stable rate.

When we look at the kinds of jobs that women have, we see that
they are quite different from the types of jobs that men have. The data

in Table 5.2 show that within each occupational category, there are some occupations that are predominantly male and others that are predominantly female. This *differential distribution of men and women in the labor force* is called **occupational sex segregation.**

Women make up 42 percent of managers, for example, which is close to their representation in the labor force. Although some would in-

Table 5.2   Employment in Occupational Categories in 2003, by Percentage Female

Occupational Category	Percentage Female	Occupational Category	Percentage Female
Managers and business		*Construction and extraction*	*2.8%*
occupations	*42.1%*	Construction, building	
Medical and health		inspectors	9.8
services	70.9	Structural iron, steel workers	0.3
Human resources	68.6	*Installers and repairers*	*4.2*
Education administrators	65.2	Coin and vending machines	21.7
Chief executive officers	23.5	Heat, air conditioner,	
Transportation, storage,		refrigeration	0.7
distribution	15.9	*Production occupations*	*31.0*
Engineering managers	10.4	Sewing machine operators	78.6
Construction managers	5.9	Textile and garment workers	74.9
Professional occupations	*56.4*	Tool and die makers	4.1
Dental hygienists	98.9	Boiler operators	2.1
Preschool, kindergarten		*Transport, material movers*	*15.3*
teachers	97.8	Packers and packagers	61.1
Licensed practical,		Bus drivers	48.4
vocational nurses	94.8	Aircraft pilots, flight engineers	3.4
Physicians	29.9	Excavate, load machine	
Lawyers	27.6	operators	1.6
Architects and engineers	14.1	*Service occupations*	*57.2*
Clergy	13.9	Transportation attendants	95.1
Sales occupations	*49.0*	Childcare workers	95.1
Models, demonstrators,		Police officers	12.4
promoters	87.2	Pest control workers	6.1
Travel agents	83.4	Firefighters	3.1
Parts sales	14.1	*Farming, fishing, forestry*	*22.0*
Sales engineers	9.5	Graders and sorters	68.0
Office and administrative		Logging workers	2.2
support	*75.9*		
Secretaries, administrative			
assistants	96.9		
Word processors, typists	93.6		
Receptionists, information			
clerks	93.2		
Couriers, messengers	17.9		
Meter readers, utilities	15.0		

Source: US Bureau of Labor Statistics 2004.

terpret this as employment equity, the picture changes when one looks at what type of managerial jobs women hold. Women are heavily overrepresented in managerial positions involved with health, human resources, and education. They are heavily underrepresented among chief executive officers and among transportation, engineering, and construction managers.

We see this same pattern in the other occupational categories. In the professions, for example, women comprise more than 94 percent of dental hygienists, preschool teachers, and licensed practical nurses, but they are less than 30 percent of the higher-paid physicians, lawyers, architects, engineers, and clergy. The fact that women make up 56 percent of all professionals must be qualified by the types of professions that they are actually employed in.

In the much-discussed service occupations, women account for more than 95 percent of transportation attendants and childcare workers, but only 12 percent of police officers and 3 percent of firefighters. In transportation, women make up 48 percent of bus drivers but only 3 percent of airline pilots. In the production (factory) occupations, women make up three-fourths of sewing machine operator and garment workers, but less than 5 percent of tool and die makers and boiler operators.

These data clearly show that occupational sex segregation is alive and well in the twenty-first century. Even more sobering is the fact that these data are improvements over what existed in the past. One common way to measure occupational sex segregation is through the Index of Dissimilarity, which ranges between 100 and 0. An index value of 100 means that all jobs are either totally male or totally female. A value of 0 means that all jobs have equal numbers of males and females. Weeden (2004) shows that the Index of Dissimilarity declined from about 48 in 1970 to 40 in 2000, a 20 percent decrease. There is still a long way to go. Although half of students in law and medical schools are now women, it will take many years to change the composition of the law and medical professions as a whole.

The area of education has also shown substantial changes. As the data in Table 5.3 show, in 1940 only about one-fourth of the population twenty-five years of age and older had graduated from high school, and less than 5 percent had graduated from college. In that same year, women were somewhat more likely than men to graduate from high school but less likely than men to graduate from college.

By 2003, things had changed dramatically. Eighty-five percent of the population had graduated from high school and 27 percent had graduated from college. High school graduation rates for men and women

Table 5.3   Percentage of Males and Females Twenty-five Years and Older Who Completed High School and College, 1940–2003

	Completed Four Years of High School or More			Completed Four Years of College or More		
Year	Males	Females	M/F Ratio[a]	Males	Females	M/F Ratio[a]
1940	22.7	26.3	0.86	5.5	3.8	1.45
1950	32.6	36.0	0.90	7.3	5.2	1.40
1960	39.5	42.5	0.93	9.7	5.8	1.67
1970	55.0	55.4	0.99	14.1	8.2	1.72
1980	69.2	68.1	1.02	20.9	13.6	1.54
1990	77.7	77.5	1.00	24.4	18.4	1.33
2000	84.2	84.0	1.00	27.8	23.6	1.18
2003	84.1	85.0	0.99	28.9	25.7	1.12

Sources: National Center for Education Statistics, http://nces.ed.gov/programs/digest/d02/tables/dt008.asp; Harvey and Anderson 2005. E.g., in 2000, 84.2 percent of males and 84.0 percent of females completed high school or more.

Note: a. Male rate divided by female rate. In 1940, the male high school graduation rate was 86 percent of the female rate.

have been equal since 1970. More important, the male/female gap in college graduation had diminished substantially. In 1940, men were 1.45 times more likely than women to graduate from college. By 2003, that gap had narrowed to 1.12. In fact, since the 1980s, more women have attended and graduated from college than men.

In spite of these developments, men and women in the United States do not get the same educations. In 2002, for example, women earned 83 percent of the bachelor's degrees in health (mostly nursing) and 79 percent of the degrees in education, but only 14 percent of the degrees in engineering (Harvey and Anderson 2005). Needless to say, engineers make a lot more money than do nurses and teachers. Although 2002 was the first year that American women earned more PhD degrees than American men, women earned two-thirds of the education PhDs and only 19 percent of the engineering PhDs (Wilson 2004).

These differences in fields of study and occupational distribution certainly have implications for gender differences in income. The data in Table 5.4 show median incomes for year-round, full-time male and female workers between 1960 and 2001. Seasonal and part-time workers, most of whom are women, are excluded from these data. In 1960, women earned only 61 percent of what men earned. By 2001 the gap had narrowed considerably so that women made 76 percent of what men made—still a substantial gap. Most of this progress occurred since 1980

Table 5.4   Median Income of Year-Round Full-Time Workers, Fifteen Years and Older, by Sex

Year	Male	Female	F/M Ratio[a]
1960	$5,368	$3,257	0.61
1970	8,966	5,323	0.59
1980	18,612	11,197	0.60
1990	27,678	19,822	0.72
2000	37,252	27,462	0.74
2001	38,275	29,215	0.76

Source: Current Population Survey, Annual Demographic Supplements, http://www.census.gov/hhes/income/histinc/p38.html.
Note: a. Female income divided by male income; e.g., in 2001, females made 76 percent of what males made.

and is due to the declining wages of men. According to Werschkul and Herman (2004, 1), "At the rate of progress achieved between 1989 and 2002, women would not achieve wage parity for more than 50 years!"

It is also important to disaggregate these data by race/ethnicity and gender group. In Table 4.7 in the previous chapter, the data for race/gender groups were presented from 1967 to 2003 and comparisons were made between races *within* a single sex; that is, the incomes of black men were compared with the incomes of white men. Using the same raw data, we can compare the incomes of the two sexes within a given race; that is, the incomes of white women were compared with the incomes of white men. These data are presented in Table 5.5.

Table 5.5   Median Income of Year-Round Full-Time Female Workers as a Percentage of Incomes of Comparable Male Workers, 1967–2003, by Race/Ethnicity

Year	Race/Ethnicity			
	White (%)	Black (%)	Hispanic (%)	Asian (%)
1967	58%	67%	—	—
1970	59	70	67%[a]	—
1980	59	79	71	—
1990	69	85	82	80%
2000	73	83	87	75
2003	70	83	87	75

Source: Calculated from data in Table 4.7.
Note: a. 1974 data. E.g., in 2003, the median income of black, female, year-round full-time workers was 83 percent of the income of comparable black male workers.

We can see that for whites, blacks, and Hispanics, the income gap between men and women has closed substantially. In 1967, white women made only 58 percent of the income of white men. By 2003, white women made 70 percent of the income of white men. The male/female gap among whites was still substantial, but it had closed. The same general patterns exist for male/female income differences among blacks and Hispanics. However, the data for Asians show that between 1990 and 2003, the income gap went from 80 percent to 75 percent: the gap has gotten larger.

The generally optimistic trends in Table 5.5 showing a steady decline in the male/female income gap may be slowing down. From 2000 to 2003, the gender gap among whites got a little larger. The black, Hispanic, and Asian gender gaps remained the same.

Since statistical data can be somewhat sterile, another way to view the income inequality between men and women is by the concept of the "Equal Pay Day," or the date each year that women have to work in order to earn the same annual income as a man. According to the Institute for Women's Policy Research (IWPR) and the National Committee on Pay Equity, women had to work until April 23, 2004, to earn the same income that a man would have earned between January 1 and December 31, 2003 (Werschkul and Herman 2004; http://www.payequity.org/day.html). Furthermore,

> Hispanic women must work almost an entire extra year, until November 22, to catch up with the earnings of the average white male in the previous year. Asian American women observe Equal Pay Day slightly earlier than all women, on March 30th. Native American women would have to work until September 12 and African American women until July 19th to catch up to the average white man's earnings from the previous year. (Werschkul and Herman 2004, 7)

Once again, there's a lot of work left to be done to achieve gender equity.

Thus far, income comparisons have been made for *all* year-round full-time workers. What happens when we control for education? In Table 4.10 in the previous chapter I presented the incomes of year-round full-time workers by race/ethnicity, gender, and education and then compared race/ethnic differences in income. Using these same data, we can compare gender differences in income in Table 5.6. In all comparisons, women have lower incomes than comparable men. For example, non-Hispanic white women with a bachelor's degree earn only 70 percent of the income of comparable men. The comparable fig-

Table 5.6   Women's Income as a Percentage of Men's Income for Year-Round Full-Time Workers in 2003, by Education and Race/Ethnicity

Education	Non-Hispanic White (%)	Black (%)	Asian (%)	Hispanic (%)
Grades 9–12	65%	88%	—	69%
High school graduate	71	80	78%	79
Some college	70	80	81	73
AA degree	76	74	77	81
Bachelor's degree +	68	82	77	82
Bachelor's degree only	70	85	84	85
Master's degree	68	80	66	83
Professional degree	69	—	—	—
PhD	75	—	—	—

Source: US Census Bureau 2004, www.ferret.bls.census.gov/macro/032004/perinc/new01_040.htm.

Note: Percentages were calculated using median income data in Table 4.10. E.g., non-Hispanic white women with a PhD earned only 75 percent of the income of comparable men.

ures for women of color with bachelor's degrees are as follows: blacks, 85 percent; Asians, 84 percent; and Hispanics, 85 percent. At each level of education, the gender gap for people of color is generally lower than it is for non-Hispanic whites. Unfortunately, the gender gap does not decrease as the level of education increases.

Some of the income differences between men and women are due to the sex-segregated labor force where women are overrepresented in low-paying jobs. What would happen if we compared male and female incomes in the same occupations? Fortunately, a recent census report allows us to do this.

Weinberg (2004) looks at the median incomes of year-round full-time workers in more than 400 different occupations that have at least 10,000 workers. In almost all of the occupations, men made more than women. The data in Table 5.7 show that in the five highest-paying occupations (physicians, dentists, CEOs, lawyers, and judges), the median income of women was only 57 percent to 73 percent that of men. In the five lowest-paying occupations (all of which are in the food service industry), women made between 81 percent and 100 percent of men's incomes.

The category of dining room and cafeteria attendants and bartender helpers was one of four occupations where the earnings of men and women were equal. The others were telecommunications line installers and repairers, meeting and convention planners, and construction trade

Table 5.7   Median Incomes of Year-Round Full-Time Workers in 1999 in High-Paying and Low-Paying Occupations, by Sex

Occupation	Male	Female	F/M Income Ratio
Highest-Paying Occupations			
Physicians and surgeons	$140,000	$88,000	.63
Dentists	110,000	68,000	.62
Chief executive officers	95,000	60,000	.63
Lawyers	90,000	66,000	.73
Judges, magistrates	88,000	50,000	.57
Lowest-Paying Occupations			
Dishwashers	14,000	12,000	.86
Dining room/cafeteria attendants, bartender helpers	15,000	15,000	1.00
Counter attendants, cafeteria, food preparation workers	16,000	13,000	.81
Combined food preparation/ serving/fast food workers	17,000	15,000	.88
Cooks	17,000	15,000	.88

Source: Weinberg 2004.

helpers. In only one occupation, hazardous materials removal workers, women actually made 110 percent of what men made.

■ Prejudice

Unlike the long tradition of research into racial prejudice, social scientists have only recently begun to systematically study prejudice toward women. Although feminist social scientists have discussed negative stereotypes and attitudes toward women for decades, this has largely been done outside of the discourse of the social psychology of prejudice. This is beginning to change.

One of the early attempts to measure prejudice toward women was the Attitudes Toward Women Scale (Spence, Helmreich, and Stapp 1973). This included agree-disagree statements like "Sons in a family should be given more encouragement to go to college than daughters" and "Women should worry less about their rights and more about becoming good wives and mothers." On the fifteen-item scale, scores ranged from 0 (traditional beliefs) to 45 (egalitarian beliefs). In a 1972 study of students at the University of Texas, for example, the mean score for men was 21.3 and the mean score for women was 24.3. Not surprisingly, men were somewhat more traditional in their beliefs than women. Those who scored low on the ATW Scale were not afraid to publicly articulate traditional stereotyped beliefs about gender roles.

By the mid-1990s it was becoming less fashionable to express these beliefs, and Spence and Hahn (1997) found that fewer and fewer people were scoring high on their ATW Scale. In their study of University of Texas students in 1992, for example, the mean score for men was 32.1 and the mean for women was 36.3. Although men were still more traditional in their views than were women, the men in the 1992 study had more egalitarian scores than did the women in the 1972 study! Several of the scale items were no longer useful since virtually everyone scored at the egalitarian end.

Twenge (1997) showed that these same trends were found in seventy-one different studies of undergraduates across the country that used the ATW Scale. She also found that southern men and women had more traditional scores than did northern men and women. Both the women's liberation movement and structural changes in the economy had strongly influenced attitudes toward women. This doesn't mean that sexism had disappeared, only that it had changed and become more complex.

A dramatic example of how unfashionable some of these traditional beliefs have become can be seen in the negative reaction to the sexist remarks of Harvard University president Lawrence Summers. In January 2005, Summers publicly suggested that the underrepresentation of women in the sciences may be due to the fact that women are biologically less capable than men in the area of math and science. The intense criticism forced him to apologize numerous times. Summers also said that Harvard would spend $50 million over ten years to encourage more women to enter the math and science fields (Healy and Rimer 2005; Jehl and Bumiller 2005).

Janet K. Swim and her colleagues (1995) approached the changing nature of prejudice by developing measures of "old-fashioned" and "modern" sexism (prejudice) toward women. The Old-Fashioned Sexism Scale included traditional items of stereotyped attitudes toward women like those in the ATW Scale.

The Modern Sexism Scale, taking its cue from some of the "new prejudice" literature discussed in the previous chapter on race, included questions that tapped a more current set of negative attitudes toward women. It included statements such as

"Women often miss out on good jobs due to sexual discrimination."
"It is easy to understand the anger of women's groups in America."

"Government and news media have been showing more concern about the treatment of women than is warranted by women's actual experience."

A prejudiced person would disagree with the first two items and agree with the third. These items are considered to be examples of modern sexism because "they support the maintenance of the status quo of gender inequality" (Swim and Campbell 2001, 221).

Although there is some correlation between these two measures, scoring high on the Old-Fashioned Sexism Scale didn't necessarily mean that you would score high on the Modern Sexism Scale, and vice versa. Swim and her colleagues argue that the two scales measure two different types of prejudice. The Neosexism Scale (Tougas et al. 1995), developed in Canada, is another attempt to measure this new form of prejudice.

The Ambivalent Sexism Inventory (Glick and Fiske 1996) also tries to make sense out of the changing nature of prejudice toward women. Previous attempts to measure sexism focused on attitudes with negative or hostile affect, such as "Most women interpret innocent remarks or acts as being sexist." Glick and Fiske also include a "benevolent sexism" subscale, which is "a set of interrelated attitudes toward women that are sexist in terms of viewing women stereotypically and in restricted roles, but that are subjectively positive in feeling tone" (491). Examples of benevolent sexism would be the following: "In a disaster, women ought to be rescued before men," and "A good woman should be set on a pedestal by her man" (Glick and Fiske 2001, 118). People who express benevolent sexism have positive attitudes toward women as long as women agree to stay in their place. The authors argue that these two types of sexism often coexist within the same individual.

The important point to take away from this discussion is that prejudice toward women is a complex phenomenon. A person can be prejudiced even if he or she doesn't endorse traditional gender stereotypes and even if he or she believes that a man is not complete without a woman. These beliefs also reinforce the inequality associated with patriarchy.

▇ Discrimination

Although public opinion polls show that most Americans believe that discrimination against women is a thing of the past, the evidence shows otherwise. The income data presented earlier in this chapter clearly showed that women earn substantially less than men, even with the same education and in the same occupation. However, though these findings should raise suspicions, they do not *prove* that discrimination exists. The pay gap could be due to sex differences in amount of time out of the labor force, level of education, subspecialization within a given job, and so on. In large-scale studies, when these factors are considered, the male/female income gap generally declines but is still substantial (Weinberg 2004; US General Accounting Office 2003). At least some of this unexplained income gap is certainly due to discrimination. Whether one examines discrimination at the individual, institutional, or structural level, the evidence clearly shows that discrimination is alive and well.

Individual Discrimination

Janet Swim and her colleagues (Swim et al. 2001) had undergraduates keep daily diaries of their observations of or experiences with sexist behavior for two weeks. The focus was on everyday experiences that did not include the media. More than one-third indicated that they had one or two experiences a week with gender-role prejudice and stereotyping; that is, they heard comments that certain roles were more appropriate for men or women or that men have greater abilities in stereotyped behavior. Thirty-two percent said that they saw or heard demeaning or derogatory comments and behavior once or twice a week. More than one-fourth experienced or observed sexual objectification.

In another campus-related study, Ehrlich, Pincus, and Lacy (1997) asked a representative sample of undergraduates if they had personally experienced ethnoviolent acts (from name-calling and graffiti to physical attacks) because of their gender during the academic year on campus. More than 11 percent of the women and less than 2 percent of the men said "yes." A quarter of the women said that they had been victims of sexual harassment on campus.

The three military academies run by the Department of Defense are also not immune from sexual misconduct. A recent study of students found that more than half of the women and 14 percent of the men said that they had been sexually assaulted while at the academies. More than two-thirds of the assaults were not reported to campus authorities, in part (according to the study respondents) because authorities were often less than sympathetic to the victims (Hirsch and Knight 2005).

The workplace is another common place in which to experience discrimination. In 2003, the Equal Employment Opportunity Commission (2004b, 2004c) received 13,566 complaints of sexual harassment on the job and 24,362 complaints of other forms of discrimination. Previous research has shown that the EEOC will find between a quarter and one-fifth of these complaints to be legally valid (Pincus 2003).

Social psychologists have also conducted studies where subjects are asked to evaluate the resumes or work experiences of anonymous people. The resumes and work experiences would be the same except that one had a female name and the other had a male name. Men are generally given higher ratings than women, even with the same resume (see Swim and Campbell 2001 for a review). It is likely that this male bias also spills into the workplace.

Institutional Sex Discrimination

In spite of all the laws on the books, there are still many examples of institutional sex discrimination. Although women can attend government-run military academies and can serve on combat ships and planes, the US Army still doesn't permit them to be in front-line combat units or in noncombat units that "collocate" with (i.e., serve alongside) all-male combat units. The reasons for the anti-collocation policy, according to conservative columnist Cal Thomas (2004, 23A), include "unit cohesion, increases in sex harassment, rape and pregnancy, and the social revulsion most feel about seeing women wounded or killed in combat." This is institutional discrimination. Although many women have been killed and injured in the Iraq war, the chaotic circumstances there make it impossible to determine what is a combat position and what is not.

Because the armed forces were running short of male soldiers in Iraq in fall 2004, some high-ranking members of the armed forces were beginning to discuss the possibility of including women in Forward Support Units, which supply combat units. A substantial public controversy developed about whether this was consistent with rules against collocation. Thomas (2004, 23A) wrote that changing the collocation policy would be "a bad idea that is not in the ultimate interest of women, men or the strength of the armed forces" (also see Scarborough 2004).

Institutional gender discrimination has also been found in police departments throughout the United States. In 2004, for example, the Los Angeles Police Department (LAPD) finally settled a gender bias suit that went back to the 1980s. The plaintiffs, fifteen female and two male officers, alleged that they were fondled, ridiculed, and harassed by other officers and then retaliated against when they complained. The problem was so serious that the LAPD instituted reforms in 1997— which both sides agreed had positive effects. The main issue was money. Finally, the LAPD agreed to pay $3.6 million to the plaintiffs and their lawyers (Morin and Garrison 2004).

Organized religion provides numerous examples of institutional discrimination. The Catholic Church doesn't allow women to be priests, Orthodox Jews don't allow women to be rabbis, and Islam doesn't allow women to be imams. It would be possible to write an entire book on institutional discrimination in religion, but these are some prominent examples.

When large multinational corporations display the same patterns of mistreating women, this is also institutional discrimination. The year 2004 found several Wall Street investment companies entering into multimillion-dollar out-of-court settlements (without acknowledging guilt) in sex discrimination cases. The industry itself is still dominated by males. In 2004, 80 percent of the executive managers and 70 percent of the investment bankers, brokers, and traders were white males (McGeehan 2004a).

In July 2004, the investment firm Morgan Stanley agreed to a $54 million arrangement to settle a class action case (McGeehan 2004a, 2004b; Gibson 2004). Six years earlier, Allison Sheieffelin, a bond saleswoman who was earning $1.5 million annually, sued Morgan Stanley for being denied a promotion to managing director and then being fired for insubordination when she complained. She also said that after a dinner for a special client that she had arranged, she was put into a cab when the men took the client to a strip club. There were also instances of workplace strip-teases and breast-shaped cakes.

The EEOC agreed to handle the case and found statistical patterns of discrimination against women at Morgan Stanley in terms of pay, promotion, and career opportunities. The case was expanded to include all 340 women who were employed at the investment bank section of Morgan Stanley since 1996, and the EEOC took the corporation to court.

The morning the trial was set to begin, lawyers for Morgan Stanley agreed to a settlement. Sheieffelin received $12 million. As well, $40 million was put into an account for the other women, whose cases would be settled by a special master. Any leftover funds would go toward programs encouraging women to enter the investment field. Finally, $2 million would be spent on diversity training and oversight.

Two other large investment firms were involved in multimillion-dollar settlements. More than 900 of the 2,800 female employees of Merrill Lynch and Company brought sex discrimination and sexual harassment charges against the company in the late 1990s. After a long series of arbitrations, Merrill Lynch paid out over $100 million in separate settlements by the spring of 2004. Responding to a $2.2 million settlement paid to Hydie Sumner in April 2004, a spokesman for Merrill Lynch stated: "The firm described in the panel's decision is not today's Merrill Lynch. We agree, and regret, that nearly a decade ago there was inappropriate behavior in the San Antonio office. It should not have occurred and would not be tolerated today" (*Diversity News* 2004a; Sachdev 2004). More than 1,900 female employees of the firm Salomon Smith Barney have filed and settled complaints of sex discrimination and harassment. The complaints began in 1985, before Smith Barney acquired Shearson American Express. The Garden City, New York, office of American Express had what was called a "boom boom room" in the basement where male employees drank and participated in what was called fraternity-house behavior. In addition to this hostile atmosphere, female brokers were discriminated against in terms of the accounts they received and the territory they were in charge of. The resulting 1,900 sex discrimination suits filed by female employees from offices around the country were submitted to arbitration before they were settled (Weinberg 2002; Spiro 1996).

One can't help but wonder what other types of sex discrimination are taking place on Wall Street. *New York Times* writer Patrick McGeehan (2004a, C7) was probably too kind when he wrote, "The problem has been that the men in charge do not seem to recognize the inequalities in their operations until they are presented with a critical analysis of the numbers."

But it's not just Wall Street. Five days after the Morgan Stanley settlement was announced, the Boeing Company entered into its own multimillion-dollar settlement of charges of sex discrimination against 29,000 nonexecutive women at three of its aircraft plants in Washington state. Boeing had an unwritten policy whereby women who were employed at low-wage entry-level jobs would never receive the salaries earned by men. The suit involved allegations of discrimination in pay, promotion, and access to overtime. The cost to Boeing was between $40.6 million and $72.5 million (Ortiz 2004a).

Although I have focused here mainly on examples of successful litigation, these settlements pale in comparison with a class-action lawsuit against Wal-Mart alleging sex discrimination against 1.6 million women workers. The suit alleges that the women were paid less and promoted less often than men. In 2004, a federal judge ruled that the case can move forward in the courts. Stay tuned.

Structural Discrimination

Much of the sex-segregated labor force described in Table 5.2 earlier in this chapter can be attributed to structural discrimination. Many male-dominated occupations have entrance standards and/or performance standards that tend to favor men. The long hours required in many up-scale law firms make it impossible for women (or men) to have anything approaching a normal family life. Since women tend to have more responsibility for children than men, these long hours would have a disproportionate impact on them. To the extent that golf and squash are important networking activities for corporate executives, women would again be disadvantaged. The camaraderie/male bonding atmosphere that is so prevalent among police officers and firefighters would also disadvantage women. These standards may not have arisen to harm women, but they have that effect. Once again, it is important to realize that structural discrimination may well exist *in addition to* more intentional individual and institutional discrimination.

In another subtle example, Linda Babcock and Sara Laschever (2003) report that although new male and female hires are offered similar starting salaries, males tend to be better negotiators and so may obtain better starting salaries than women. Employers, wanting to pay *all* employees as little as possible, regardless of sex, simply accept this state of affairs. This is structural discrimination because women get unequal pay for doing the same work.

The world of education also has a great deal of structural discrimination. Competitive and individualistic pedagogical techniques in math and science classes throughout the educational system favor males over females due to differential socialization practices. There is growing evidence that women and girls learn better in more cooperative settings. The lack of female role models among the faculty in many disciplines also hurts women.

In higher education, the relatively small number of women faculty results in greater demands on their time for advising students and participation in committee work. This, in turn, reduces the amount of time women faculty have to spend on research, which is all-important for promotion and tenure decisions.

* * *

This chapter has shown that women are still a subordinate group in the United States. In spite of some modest progress, women still have lower incomes and lower-paying jobs than men. In addition, women are the targets of prejudice and intentional discrimination. Many attitudinal and institutional changes must still be made in order to achieve true gender equality.

6

Sexual Orientation

INDIVIDUALS HAVE BEEN HAVING SEXUAL RELATIONS WITH SAME-sex partners for centuries. The Bible and the Koran discuss this fact, although critically. In fact, homosexual liaisons were seen as normal and acceptable behavior among the ancient Greeks, and in many other societies throughout history were usually viewed as a behavior in which some people participated rather than as a separate status. In some societies homosexual behavior was condemned; in others it was not.

It wasn't until the second half of the nineteenth century that homosexuality began to be discussed in a way that defined one's sense of being; that is, that someone is a "homosexual" if he or she engages in homosexual behavior (Katz 1995; Baird 2001). In fact, the noun forms of *homosexual* and *heterosexual* were popularized in the 1890s and probably weren't even used in the English language prior to the 1860s.

■ Terminology

Like the concepts surrounding class, race, and gender that we discussed earlier, there is often disagreement about the terminology surrounding **sexual orientation,** *which is determined by those to whom we are attracted sexually, physically, and emotionally.* This is preferred to the term *sexual preference* because the latter suggests that there is a choice about whether or not we are attracted to people of the same or opposite sex. Today, most researchers believe that sexual orientation is probably something that an individual is born with.

Heterosexual *refers to those who are sexually, physically, and emotionally attracted to people of the opposite sex.* The term **homosexual** *refers to those who are sexually, physically, and emotionally attracted to people of the same sex.* Homosexual males are often called **gay males**, and homosexual females are often called **lesbians**. However, **gay** is also used as an umbrella term to refer to all homosexuals, and the term **straight** refers to heterosexuals. **Bisexual** *refers to individuals who are sexually, physically, and emotionally attracted to both same- and opposite-sex partners.* In the previous chapter, we defined **transgendered** people as *those whose gender identity doesn't match their physiological sex.*

All of these different categories of people are part of the general discussion of sexual orientation. In fact, it is common to refer to non-heterosexuals as the **GLBT** (or LGBT) population (i.e., gays, lesbians, bisexuals, and transgendered people) since they share many common issues. I will use this terminology in the rest of the chapter.

GLBT people may or may not acknowledge their sexual orientation to themselves and others. Someone who is **in the closet** *has not revealed his or her GLBT sexual orientation to others.* The process of **coming out** means that *an individual has revealed his or her GLBT sexual orientation to others.* Coming out is usually a process rather than a discrete event since individuals may acknowledge their sexual orientation to a close friend before telling other acquaintances or their families.

The concepts of homosexual, heterosexual, and bisexual may seem to be straightforward, but there are substantial difficulties in determining who is in what category. Although the concepts are all defined in terms of whom one is attracted to, attraction is not the same thing as actually having sex with that person. **Sexual behavior** *refers to whom we have sex with.* This raises some important questions. Is it necessary to have a sexual relationship with a same-sex partner in order to be defined as homosexual, or is *attraction* to a same-sex partner sufficient to warrant the label homosexual? For example, can a Catholic priest who is attracted to other males but who remains celibate be called gay, or would he have to engage in sex with another male to earn the gay label?

Another conceptual problem is about the timing and frequency of homosexual behaviors. In the islands of Melanesia, part of the rite of passage for boys is to have fellatio with older men. Eating another man's sperm is seen as a way to gain masculinity and bond with their male ancestors. After the initiation, most men are exclusively heterosexual until they have to initiate younger men (Heyl 2003). We may describe this as a kind of institutionalized homosexuality, though the Melanesians would simply see it as normal male behavior.

In our own society, is a forty-five-year-old man gay, or straight, if his only homosexual act was an experimental one-night stand with another boy when both were teenagers? Is a thirty-five-year-old married woman a lesbian if she had a six-month lesbian relationship when she was twenty-five? What about a fifty-year-old man who first came out in his late forties? Can we use the same label to describe these different behaviors?

More than fifty years ago, Alfred Kinsey and his colleagues (1948, 1953) documented the variety of sexual experiences by rating people according to the following scale:

0 – exclusively heterosexual; no homosexual experiences
1 – predominantly heterosexual; only incidental homosexual experiences
2 – predominantly heterosexual; more than incidental homosexual experiences
3 – equally heterosexual and homosexual
4 – predominantly homosexual; more than incidental heterosexual experiences
5 – predominantly homosexual; only incidental heterosexual experiences
6 – exclusively homosexual; no heterosexual experiences

Where on this scale must someone fall to be called homosexual (or bisexual or heterosexual)? As we have seen in previous chapters, the answer to this question is philosophical and cultural, not scientific. The concept of sexual orientation, like the concepts of class, race, and gender, is socially constructed.

The answer, however, is important in determining the prevalence of homosexuality in the general population. According to Kinsey et al., for example, about 6 percent of adult males and 3 percent of adult females were exclusively homosexual (#6) in the late 1950s and early 1960s. Under a broader definition (#4–6) 10 percent of males were exclusively or predominantly homosexual. Which figure should be used?

Lee Ellis (1996) takes a similar approach in trying to determine the prevalence of homosexuality in the United States during more recent times. Using the broad criterion of ever having a same-sex fantasy or sexual desire, 25–30 percent of males and 10–20 percent of females would be defined as gay. According to the more restrictive criterion of ever having a same-sex erotic experience to orgasm, 5–10 percent of the males and 1–3 percent of the females would be gay. Using the strictest criterion, having more or less exclusive erotic preference for one's own sex, only 1–4 percent of the males and less than 1 percent of the females would qualify. Ellis also argues that these same patterns can be found in studies in other countries. Male rates are always substantially higher than female rates.

So far, we have discussed whom people are attracted to and have sex with. There is yet another issue to contend with. **Sexual identification** *is what people call themselves.* Men who are attracted to other men and who have sexual relations with other men still don't always define themselves as homosexual. Many male prisoners, for example, have sex with other male prisoners but define themselves as straight. Only the "penetrated" male prisoners tend to be defined as gay. Also, some black men, who are said to be "on the down low" because they have public heterosexual relationships with women and multiple secret relationships with other men, insist on defining themselves as straight rather than gay or bisexual (King 2004). Is it necessary for people to define themselves as gay in order to be gay?

It is extremely difficult to answer what seem to be simple questions: Who is gay? How many people are gay? The answers always have to be qualified by another question: What do you mean by gay? There is no "objective" answer since labels are always socially constructed. Despite this, we do have some estimates of how many people participate in different kinds of sexual behaviors. What difference does it make if the behavior is labeled gay or not gay?

There are two additional concepts that are important in understanding sexual orientation. **Homophobia** *refers to the fear and hatred of those who love and sexually desire people of the same sex.* This refers to an anti-gay set of attitudes and an ideology that are major problems in the United States. As we will see, homophobia can lead to hate crimes and other forms of discrimination.

Heterosexism, in contrast, *refers to a system of oppression against the GLBT population.* Prejudice and ideology are one part of oppression, but there is more. Heterosexuals have certain privileges that gays don't, like being able to have a picture of one's partner on one's desk at work without being hassled, or being able to hold hands with one's partner in public without having to worry about verbal harassment or physical assault. There also are discriminatory laws that prevent gays from marrying and that don't protect their civil rights. Hate crimes and violence are also part of heterosexism. We will explore these issues more in the following sections.

▨ Descriptive Statistics

In previous chapters I provided statistics on income, employment, and education that were collected by various agencies of the federal government. These data all show substantial inequalities between the dominant and subordinate groups. For a variety of reasons, it is impossible to obtain comparable data for sexual orientation.

First, the federal government doesn't collect data on groups with different sexual orientations. Even if it did, many closeted gays would not acknowledge their sexual orientations on the census forms. Finally, most of the fine books on sexual orientation don't address the issue of large-scale differences in employment, occupation, income, and education.

In 1990 and 2000, the US census did provide data on gays in the Public Use Microdata Sample (PUMS), which represents 5 percent of the population. In describing the relationship of people living in households, respondents were given the option of checking off "unmarried partner." Since it also was possible to determine if these partners were of the same or opposite sex, the PUMS data shed some light on gay and lesbian couples. Although same-sex unmarried partners living in the same household are not necessarily representative of all gays and lesbians, the data are national in scope and may be the best that are available.

There are three different analyses of the 2000 census data on same-sex couples—gaydemographics.org, the Human Rights Campaign (Smith and Gates 2001), and the National Black Justice Coalition of the National Gay and Lesbian Task Force Institute (Dang and Frazier 2004). Two of the reports agree that 601,209 same-sex couples were identified in the 2000 PUMS: 304,148 male couples and 297,061 females. This represents about 1 percent of all couples who responded to the 2000 US census. Dang and Frazier (2004) put the number at "nearly 600,000." Due to undercounting caused by the reluctance of many gay couples to identify themselves as unmarried partners, Smith and Gates (2001) estimates that the true number of gay couples may be over 1.5 million.

Gaydemographics.org describes the racial distribution of same-sex couples as follows: 79 percent white, 9 percent black, 12 percent Hispanic, 2 percent Asian, and 1 percent Native American. Smith and Gates put the black percentage at 14 percent. Like other couples, most of the same-sex partners (89 percent) were of the same race. However, the rate of racially mixed same-sex partners was four times greater than in the general population.

In addition to simply describing gay and lesbian couples, the PUMS data allow them to be compared with straight couples. Unfortunately, only Dang and Frazier do this in a systematic way, and their focus is on black couples. In terms of comparisons, I will stick with these data even though they are incomplete.

The distribution of household income for gay and lesbian couples is presented in Table 6.1. There is a large range of incomes, from the very poor to the well-to-do. This is clearly inconsistent with the stereotype of all gays and lesbians being upper-middle class. The mean household income is $72,122, and the median is $57,608.

Comparative income data are presented in Table 6.2. To no one's surprise, white homosexual couples earn substantially more than black homosexual couples among both males and females. Mixed-race couples

Table 6.1   Distribution (percentage) of Household Income of Same-Sex Couples in 1999

Percent	Income
16%	0–$25,000
27	$25,100–50,000
23	$50,100–75,000
14	$75,100–100,000
7	$100,100–125,000
4	$125,100–150,000
5	$150,100–250,000
3	$250,100+
Mean	$72,122
Median	$57,608

Source: http://www.gaydemographics.org.

Table 6.2   Median Household Income in 1999 by Race, Gender, and Sexual Orientation

Race	Same-Sex Couples		Opposite-Sex Couples	
	Male	Female	Married	Cohabiting
White	$69,000	$60,000	—	—
Black	$45,000	$40,000	$51,000	$41,000
Black/other[a]	$67,000	$52,000	—	—

Source: Dang and Frazier 2004.
Note: a. Mixed-race couples with at least one black member.

having at least one black partner earned slightly less than white couples. In addition, gay men earned more than lesbians in each racial group.

Among black opposite-sex couples, those who are married earned more than same-sex couples. However, black cohabiting opposite-sex couples had similar incomes to same-sex couples. Similar comparisons for whites and mixed couples are not available.

Home ownership is another indicator of economic status. In Table 6.3, white same-sex couples are more likely to own homes than are comparable blacks (70 percent and 52 percent, respectively). Home ownership differences between gay male and lesbian couples were small. Although black married opposite-sex couples were substantially more likely to own their homes than black same-sex couples, black cohabiting couples were much less likely to own their own homes.

Gay and lesbian couples are also relatively well educated. According to gaydemographics.org, 18 percent of the couples had no high school diploma, 23 percent graduated from high school but didn't attend college, 21 percent had some college, 25 percent had a bachelor's degree, and 13 percent had postgraduate degrees. Dang and Frazier (2004) present comparative data only in terms of whether respondents had education beyond high school (Table 6.4). Mixed-race and white same-sex

Table 6.3 Home Ownership Rates for Couples in 1999 by Race, Gender, and Sexual Orientation

Race	Same-Sex Couples (%)			Opposite-Sex Couples (%)	
	Male	Female	Total	Married	Cohabiting
White	72	71	70	—	—
Black	54	50	52	68	28

Source: Dang and Frazier 2004.

Table 6.4 Percentage of Couples Who Had Education Beyond High School, by Race and Sexual Orientation

Race	Same-Sex Couples (%)	Opposite-Sex Couples (%)	
		Married	Cohabiting
Whites	67	—	—
Black	40	50	48
Black/other	71	—	—

Source: Dang and Frazier 2004.

couples were much more likely to have education beyond high school than were black same-sex couples. Black opposite-sex couples were more likely to have gone beyond high school than were black same-sex couples.

The top ten occupations for people who are part of same-sex couples are first-line supervisors of retail sales workers, truck drivers, retail salespeople, secretaries and administrative assistants, elementary and middle-school teachers, nurses, miscellaneous managers, cashiers, customer service representatives, and nursing/home health aides. Not surprisingly, there was a familiar gender division of labor in the occupations held by same-sex couples. Gay men made up 66 percent of the designers who were same-sex partners; the remaining 34 percent of designers were lesbians. Sixty-one percent of the auto mechanics, 60 percent of the truck drivers, and 57 percent of the janitors were gay men. Lesbians, in comparison, were 72 percent of the childcare workers, 68 percent of the counselors, 62 percent of the accountants, and 53 percent of the waitresses (gaydemographics.org). Remember, the base upon which these percentages were calculated is people in a particular occupation who were also members of a same-sex couple.

The data in these four tables clearly show that white same-sex couples are economically better off than comparable black couples and that gay male couples are more advantaged than lesbian couples. The data are not consistent with the stereotype that gays and lesbians are more affluent than heterosexuals. Black same-sex couples, on the whole, are *less* economically advantaged than black married opposite-sex couples. The comparisons between black same-sex couples and black cohabiting opposite-sex couples are inconsistent. These conclusions are tentative since there are no comparative data about nonblacks.

Badgett (2000) and Allegreto and Arthur (2001) have completed complex analyses of 1990 census data and several other large-scale studies. After statistically controlling for factors like education, occupation, and age, they found that the incomes of gay male unmarried partners were *lower* than the incomes of heterosexual married men. Lesbian incomes, however, were the *same* as the incomes of heterosexual married women. Looking at household income, gay male unmarried partner households earned the same or less than heterosexual married couples. Lesbian unmarried couples earned less than heterosexual married couples. Badgett (2000, 24) concludes that "lesbians, gays and bisexuals are spread throughout the range of household income distribution."

Finally, Table 6.5 looks at the percentage of couples with children living in their home. Although lesbian couples are more likely than gay

Table 6.5 **Percentage of Couples with Children in the Home, by Race, Gender, and Sexual Orientation**

	Same-Sex Couples		Opposite-Sex Couples	
Race	Male (%)	Female (%)	Married (%)	Cohabiting (%)
White	24	38	—	—
Black	46	61	69	51

Source: Dang and Frazier 2004.

male couples to have children in the home, almost one-quarter of white gay male couples and 46 percent of black gay male couples have children in the home. This certainly goes against the stereotype of childless gay and lesbian couples.

Black same-sex couples, both male and female, are more likely than comparable white couples to have children in the home. They are, however, less likely than black married couples to have children living in the home. The rate of children in the home for black opposite-sex cohabiting couples falls between the lesbian and gay male rates.

▇ Prejudice

Unlike the paucity of data about gays in the labor force, there is an abundance of data on attitudes toward gays and how things have changed over time. However, the interpretation of these data results is a "glass half empty or half full" dilemma. During the past 20–30 years, attitudes have been moving in the direction of more tolerance, but a great deal of homophobia still exists.

I will discuss two important documents about attitudes toward homosexuals. The American Enterprise Institute (AEI), one of the country's leading conservative think tanks, has issued a document titled "Attitudes About Homosexuality" that examines attitude change between the 1970s and the present (Bowman 2004). The *Los Angeles Times* has released the results of its national "Gay Issues Survey," which took place in spring 2004 (Pinkus and Richardson 2004). Taken together, these documents will help us understand how Americans think about sexual orientation.

First, the good news: American adults seem to be moving in a more tolerant direction. In 1983, 38 percent of the respondents reported that they were uncomfortable around gays. In 2004, only 20 percent reported being uncomfortable, and 56 percent said that they were comfortable. Similarly, the percentage of adults who said they were sympathetic to the gay community increased from 30 percent in 1984 to 60 percent in 2004.

Respondents also became more approving of gay rights. In 1989, 29 percent approved of gay rights and 51 percent disapproved. In 2004, however, respondents were evenly divided, with 42 percent approving and 42 percent disapproving of gay rights. They were also more likely to support laws protecting gays from job discrimination (56 percent in 1993 and 72 percent in 2004), to accept gays in the military (27 percent in 1977 and 51 percent in 2004), to vote for gay candidates (41 percent in 1985 and 59 percent in 2004), and to have their child taught by a gay elementary school teacher (27 percent in 1977 and 61 percent in 2004).

Fifty-eight percent would permit their child to play at the home of a friend with a gay parent. Finally, 58 percent agreed with the idea that love between two same-sex partners could be the same as love between opposite-sex partners, and 56 percent said that if two people are in love and committed to each other, it didn't matter if they were of the same or opposite sex.

The results of these two polls are consistent with studies of university students and their parents that show attitudes changing in the more tolerant direction (Altemeyer 2001). This is the good news.

Unfortunately, there's also bad news. Fifty-seven percent still think that same-sex relations are against God's will, and a slight plurality (48 percent to 46 percent) believe that same-sex relations are morally wrong. Less than one-quarter support gay marriage, and over half support a constitutional amendment defining marriage as being between a man and a woman. Fifty-two percent oppose legal adoptions by gays.

Respondents are sharply divided when it comes to dealing with their own children. A slim plurality would not hire a gay babysitter (45 percent to 43 percent) and would not permit their child to read a book that contains a same-sex couple (45 percent to 44 percent). Two-thirds would be upset if they found that their own child was gay. In terms of political power, 32 percent felt that gays had too much, 32 percent said that they had the right amount, and only 20 percent said that they had too little. Fifty-five percent said that the media gave too much coverage to gay issues.

When these data are disaggregated to see how demographic factors affect attitudes, there are some consistent findings. Men, older people, fundamentalist Christians (those who literally interpret the Bible), and political conservatives are the most likely to display anti-gay prejudice.

Women, younger people, Catholics, non-Catholic Christians, and political liberals tend to have more tolerant attitudes toward gays.

A 2005 survey looked at how views on gay marriage and civil unions are influenced by religion. Only 25 percent of evangelical Protestants supported gay marriage or civil unions, compared to 53 percent of mainline Protestants, 55 percent of Catholics, and 84 percent of Jews. Sixty-nine percent of those who described themselves as unaffiliated supported gay marriage or civil unions (D'Arcy 2005).

Studies of the attitudes of college students, summarized by Hinrichs and Rosenberg (2002), have found that the two most important factors predicting attitudes toward gays and lesbians are sex role attitudes and interpersonal relations with homosexuals. Students who have liberal sex role attitudes have more positive feelings toward gays than those with more traditional sex role attitudes. In addition, students who have positive interpersonal relationships with at least one homosexual will have more positive feelings toward gays than those who don't know any gays or who have negative relationships.

Although neither the AEI nor the *Los Angeles Times* report discusses race, Lewis (2003) reviews thirty-one studies that compare black and white attitudes toward homosexuals. He found that blacks are more likely than whites to agree with the following statements:

"Homosexual relations are always wrong."
"AIDS is God's punishment to homosexuals."
"Pro-gay books should be removed from the public library."
"Gays should not be permitted to give a public talk in the community."

In terms of employment issues, Lewis found that blacks and whites had the same attitudes about employing a gay college professor, firing gay teachers, hiring gays in five different occupations, and allowing gays to serve in the military. Blacks were, however, more likely than whites to support laws preventing anti-gay discrimination.

According to Lewis, some of the anti-gay attitudes among blacks are due to their low levels of education and high levels of membership in fundamentalist Christian churches. When these and other factors are statistically controlled, the gap in black/white hostility to gays shrinks but the greater black than white support of gay employment rights grows. In other words, a blanket statement that blacks are more homophobic than whites is oversimplified.

How are we to interpret the broad findings that American public opinion is moving in a more tolerant direction? Pinkus and Richardson

(2004), who analyzed the *Los Angeles Times* poll, are quite clear: "The poll shows that the public appears to be more accepting and more tolerant of people in this country who are gays and lesbians than they were even just a decade ago" (1). Bowman (2004), author of the AEI report, concurs.

Many social psychologists who study anti-gay prejudice are not so sure that tolerance is increasing. Morrison and Morrison (2002) acknowledge that scores on two major traditional (or old-fashioned) anti-gay prejudice scales have declined. Both male and female college students now score below the neutral point (i.e., on the nonprejudiced side) on the Attitudes Toward Lesbian Scale and the Attitudes Toward Gay Men Scale (together referred to as the ATLG). These two scales ask respondents to indicate whether they agree or disagree with the following types of statements:

> "Gay men should be avoided whenever possible."
> "Gay women should not be allowed to work with children."
> "Those who support the rights of gay men are probably gay themselves."

Morrison and Morrison offer several possible explanations of the declining scores on these traditional prejudice scales. Respondents may be growing more tolerant, or they may be concealing their true feelings, or the sample may be statistically biased since most studies are done on college students.

The authors, however, prefer a different explanation: "It is possible that scales such as the ATLG examine a specific type of homonegativity; one that many college and university students no longer endorse. . . . Students may evidence low levels of homonegativity on old-fashioned measures not because they possess favorable attitudes toward gay men and lesbians, but simply because they consider old-fashioned measures to be anachronistic" (Morrison and Morrison 2002, 17–18).

Morrison and Morrison instead argue that this old-fashioned prejudice has been replaced by a new form of prejudice that can be measured by their Modern Homonegativity Scale (MHS). This new scale contains twelve items, including the following:

> "Many gay men use their sexual orientation so that they can obtain special privileges."
> "Lesbians should stop shoving their lifestyle down other people's throats."

"If gay men want to be treated like everyone else, then they need to
stop making such a fuss about their sexuality/culture."

This modern anti-gay prejudice focuses on the belief that gays and lesbians make illegitimate and unnecessary demands, that discrimination
against homosexuals is a thing of the past, and that homosexuals exag-
gerate the importance of their sexual orientation. In a series of studies
on Canadian college students, Morrison and Morrison (2002) show that
the patterns of responses to the MHS are distinct from the answers to
the ATL/ATG scales. In other words, it may be that one type of anti-gay
prejudice is simply being replaced by another that fits in with the
twenty-first century. This approach to the changing nature of anti-gay
prejudice is similar to the studies of race and gender prejudice that have
been discussed in previous chapters.

On the other hand, it's sobering to remember that vicious anti-gay
prejudice is still alive and well, especially among conservative Christian fundamentalists (Moser 2005). On September 12, 2004, for example, conservative televangelist Jimmy Swaggart was discussing homosexuals during one of his broadcasts and said, "I've never seen a man in
my life I wanted to marry. . . . I'm going to be blunt and plain. If one
ever looks at me like that, I'm going to kill him and tell God he died"
(*Diversity News* 2004c). The audience laughed and applauded. Swaggart later said that he was trying to be humorous and that he was only
using the "killing" expression figuratively.

Discrimination

Given the strong incentives for many GLBT people to remain in the
closet as well as the lack of systematic data collection, it is difficult to
be precise about the amount of discrimination based on sexual orientation that takes place. Verbal harassment is probably too frequent to even
count. Among middle and high school children, for example, it is common to use terms like *fag* and *dike* to tease and harass *heterosexual*
classmates who are not members of the "in crowd." Known GLBT
classmates also are the targets of verbal harassment. Gerstenfeld (2004)
estimates that as many as 80 percent of GLBT children and adults will
be verbally harassed in any given year.

Verbal harassment is the most common form of **individual discrimination** against gays. A recent national survey by the Gay, Lesbian,
and Straight Education Network (2004) showed that 91.5 percent of gay

and lesbian students had heard homophobic remarks and 84.5 percent reported being verbally harassed because of their sexual orientation. Physical violence is also common. The same survey showed that 58 percent of gay students had their property damaged and 39.1 percent had been physically harassed (i.e., shoved or pushed). Sixty-four percent said that they felt unsafe at school, and 29 percent had missed at least one day of school for safety reasons.

Since the federal government began collecting data on hate crimes in 1991, 12,000 anti-gay hate crimes have been reported to the police. In 2002 alone, 1,294 anti-gay hate crimes were reported. This accounted for 16.7 percent of all reported hate crimes that year (Human Rights Campaign 2004b). Everyone agrees that this is only the tip of the iceberg. Gerstenfeld (2004) estimates that 20–25 percent of GLBT people are victims of a hate crime each year. Studies have shown that anti-gay victimization follows predictable patterns—men more than women, people of color more than whites, threats and physical violence more than property crime. The perpetrators of anti-gay hate crimes are most likely to be young, lone males.

In terms of individual discrimination in employment, gays are not protected by federal civil rights laws. Consequently, data on anti-gay discrimination are not available from the Equal Employment Opportunity Commission. Similarly, gays are not protected from employment discrimination by state and local laws in most areas. Surveys have shown that more than two-fifths of gays have said that they had been harassed at work, had been denied a promotion, or were forced to quit because of their sexual orientation (Edwards 2003).

Juan Battle and his colleagues (2002) conducted a survey of 2,645 black gays who attended Black Pride events in the summer of 2002. They asked respondents about their experiences with race and sexual orientation discrimination in a variety of areas. Respondents were asked to say if most of the experiences had been negative, positive, or equally negative and positive.

In terms of experiencing some type of racial discrimination in mixed-race GLBT organizations and bars, black GLBT people reported more negative than positive experiences. In terms of racial discrimination in mixed-race community events and personal relations, they reported more positive than negative experiences. Almost half of the respondents said that racism was a problem among white GLBT people.

Respondents were also asked to evaluate homophobic experiences that they had in the black community. In terms of homophobic experiences in heterosexual black organizations and with families and friends, respondents reported more positive than negative experiences. In terms of black churches and religious organizations, they reported more negative than positive experiences. Two-thirds of the respondents said that homophobia was a problem in the black community.

This study indicates the complexity of experiences with discrimination for black GLBT individuals. Aside from problems with black religious organizations, black GLBT respondents were more likely to report *racial* discrimination from white GLBT people than *anti-gay* discrimination from the black heterosexual community.

When it comes to institutional discrimination against GLBT people, the situation in the United States is still ugly. Though legal discrimination on the basis of race and gender has been declining, discrimination on the basis of sexual orientation is still common. GLBT people are not protected under federal civil rights legislation or regulations. In spring 2004, in fact, the Bush administration removed sexual-orientation language from the website and forms of the Office of the Special Council, which is supposed to provide some protection for federal employees (*Diversity News* 2004b). Only fourteen states include protection for gay men and lesbians in their civil rights acts, and twenty-nine states include sexual orientation in their hate crime legislation (Human Rights Campaign 2004a, b).

Prior to 1991, the military simply excluded open homosexuals. The Clinton administration "liberalized" this policy by instituting the "Don't ask, don't tell" rule. This meant that gays could serve if they were discreet (i.e., not public) about their sexual orientation. Nevertheless, the Center for the Study of Sexual Minorities in the Military reported that more than 10,000 gays and lesbians have been discharged from the military since 1997, the year they started counting. In 2004 alone, 653 were discharged (*Baltimore Sun* 2004). Gay soldiers are unlikely to file harassment suits since that would require them to come out, which would in turn lead to their discharge.

In addition to civil rights concerns, this anti-gay institutionalized discrimination is hurting the military itself. During the first half of 2005 the various branches of the military failed to meet their recruitment quotas, in part due to the war in Iraq. At the same time, at least twenty Arab-speaking gay soldiers were discharged. The Government Accounting Office reported that it cost more than $200 million to recruit and train new soldiers to replace the 10,000 gays that were discharged (Files 2005).

Other federal agencies under the Bush administration have also engaged in anti-gay actions. Consider the controversy over the PBS-funded program *Postcards from Buster* in the winter of 2005. Buster is an animated character who interacts with live people on the show for preschoolers that is supposed to promote diversity. During a program on maple syrup, a girl introduces Buster to her two mothers. This was too much for Secretary of Education Margaret Spellings, who dissociated the department from supporting the show. She also suggested that the producers return any federal money that was used to make the program. As a result of the controversy, only 18 of the 349 PBS affiliates aired the program (Zurawik 2005).

Another federal agency objected to the title of a workshop, "Suicide Prevention Among Gays, Lesbians, Bisexuals, and Transgendered Individuals." The workshop was to be part of a conference sponsored by the Suicide Prevention Resource Center in 2005. Organizers were informed that the head of the Substance Abuse and Mental Health Service Administration would not attend the conference unless the reference to GLBT individuals was removed from the workshop's title. The workshop was renamed "Suicide Prevention in Vulnerable Populations," but the term "sexual orientation" couldn't even be included in the workshop description (Vanderburgh 2005).

Laws regarding marriage and civil unions are other examples of institutional discrimination. Forty states have laws that specifically ban same-sex marriage. In the 2004 presidential election, voters in eleven states approved constitutional amendments that define marriage as a union between a man and a woman. Only Massachusetts licenses same-sex marriage, and only Vermont and Connecticut recognize civil unions. California, Hawaii, and New Jersey have more limited domestic partner legislation. At the federal level, the Defense of Marriage Act of 1996 defined marriage as between a man and a woman, so same-sex partners are ineligible for a wide range of federal benefits. With the support of the Bush administration, conservatives are also promoting a constitutional amendment that would ban gay marriages. The amendment states: "Marriage in the United States shall consist only of the union of a man and a woman. Neither this constitution nor the constitution of any state, nor state or federal law, shall be construed to require that marital status or the legal incidents thereof be conferred upon unmarried couples or groups" (Human Rights Campaign 2004a, b).

This would be the first time that a constitutional amendment would limit rights to an entire group of people. In addition to preventing same-sex couples of the emotional benefits of marriage, the laws in most states prevent gays and lesbians from having the legal and economic rights that go along with marriage in terms of inheritance, children, hospital visitation, and more than 1,000 other benefits.

The marriage controversy even filters down to school textbooks on health. Two major publishers—Holt, Rinehart, and Winston, and McGraw Hill—had used terms like "married partners" and "when two people marry." Several members of the Texas Board of Education said that because of this wording, the books could not be used in Texas (the nation's second-largest buyer of school textbooks) since it is contrary to a state law banning gay civil unions and marriage. After the publishers agreed to use phrases like "husband and wife" and "when a man and a woman marry," the board approved the books for use in Texas (Associated Press 2004).

Institutional discrimination can also be seen in organized religions. Both the Jewish and Christian versions of the Bible denounce homosexuality as a sin. In some religions (Mormons and Orthodox Jews), gays and lesbians are banished from the family and the community. In others, there is a "hate the sin, love the sinner" approach whereby homosexuals can't be officials of the church/temple/mosque but are still accepted into the community. In 2004 the fundamentalist Southern Baptists split off from the main Baptist organization in protest of the latter's more liberal stand toward homosexuality (Human Rights Campaign 2004a). These anti-gay religious institutions are one major cause of the strong homophobic ideology that exists in the United States.

In December 2003, Baylor University, the nation's largest Baptist university, revoked the financial aid of seminary student Matt Bass when administrators learned he was gay. Unable to continue his studies, Bass withdrew from the university (Human Rights Campaign 2004a).

In 2005 the United Church of Christ became the first mainstream Christian denomination to support gay marriage. A few other religious communities, including Reform Judaism, Unitarians, Episcopalians, Presbyterians, Evangelical Lutherans, and the Metropolitan Community Church, sanction same-sex unions (*New York Times* News Service 2005). Most contemporary religions contain groups trying to liberalize their policies toward gays and lesbians (Baird 2001; D'Arcy 2005).

It is difficult to document institutional discrimination in the world of work, although it clearly remains a serious problem. The subtitle of a *Business Week* article, for example, states, "Gays are making huge strides everywhere but in the executive suite" (Edwards 2003, 64). Sandals Resorts International prohibits gay couples from staying at its couples-only resorts in the Caribbean. In an unapologetic explanation, Sandals states: "While it is understandable that some might have questions about the guest policies at Sandals, we want to underscore that everyone is welcome at our ultra all-inclusive Beaches Resorts (regardless of marital/family status or sexual orientation)" (Johnson 2004b).

Given the continuing high incidence of anti-gay individual and institutional discrimination, it becomes somewhat less important to discuss **structural discrimination** (i.e., neutral policies that have negative impacts on gays). In the race and gender chapters, I emphasized that in spite of the decline in intentional individual and institutional discrimination, structural discrimination was still important. With sexual orientation, intentional discrimination is still dominant.

One example of anti-gay structural discrimination would be elementary school assignments asking children to draw pictures of their families. In this seemingly innocuous assignment, teachers expect children to draw a man and/or a woman. The children of gay parents, however, are put in the position of "outing" their families to the entire class and bringing anti-gay harassment onto themselves. Unless the teacher is sensitive to these issues, this could cause real problems for both the child and the family (Hofmann 2005).

Of course, there is still a great deal of individual discrimination in the field of education. In one example of an outrageously insensitive teacher, a Louisiana elementary school student was punished for telling a classmate that his mother was gay. When one child asked Marcus McLaurin about his mother and father, Marcus replied that he has two mothers. During the brief discussion, Marcus said that his mothers were gay, meaning that "gay is when a girl likes another girl" (Stepp 2003, C10). The teacher overheard the conversation and criticized Marcus for using a bad word. The teacher then filled out an official "behavior report," writing, in part, "This kind of discussion is not acceptable in my room. I feel that parents should explain things of this nature to their own children in their own way" (Stepp 2003, C10).

Before leaving the topic of anti-gay discrimination, it's important to acknowledge that there is some progress in trying to combat intentional individual and institutional discrimination. In 2003 the US Supreme Court overturned the anti-sodomy laws in Texas that had outlawed oral and anal sex. The *Lawrence v. Texas* decision also invalidated anti-sodomy laws in fourteen other states. According to Richard Goldstein (2003), "It's the most momentous gay rights decision in American history. Justice Anthony Kennedy's language explicitly gives homosexuals the right to have intimate relationships . . . in private between consenting adults."

In spring and summer 2004, there was a lot of activity in state legislatures around the issues of hate crimes and civil rights. In the workplace, 7,149 private companies and educational institutions offered same-sex domestic partner benefits in 2003, an 18 percent increase from the previous year. This includes 40 percent of Fortune 500 companies (Johnson 2004a).

The Human Rights Campaign has also reported progress. Since 1996, it has been issuing an annual list of the best and worst companies for GLBT employees. It rates large corporations "on a scale of 0 to 100 percent on seven criteria including: health insurance for same-sex domestic partners; recognize and support GLBT employee groups; marketing to the GLBT market; and including the words 'sexual orientation' in their primary non-discrimination policy" (Davis 2004). In the 2004 list, fifty-six corporations received perfect scores, double the number in 2003.

When it comes to television, there is both good news and bad news. The good news is that the number of gay and lesbian characters in scripted cable TV dramas is, according to the Gay and Lesbian Alliance Against Defamation (GLAAD), increasing (Welch 2004). Fifteen gay males, nine lesbians, and two bisexuals were regular characters on cable dramas in 2004. In contrast, only five gay males and one lesbian were regular characters on network dramas that year, the lowest number since GLAAD began keeping statistics in 1996. In addition, most of the characters are white and middle-class and are often portrayed in stereotypical ways (Weinraub and Rutenberg 2003).

In December 2004, CBS and NBC refused to air a thirty-second commercial by the United Church of Christ emphasizing inclusiveness. In the ad, a bouncer-type person who was standing in front of a church allowed white mixed-sex couples to enter but turned away people of color and same-sex couples. The ad ended with the words, "Jesus didn't turn away people. Neither do we." The networks' explanation was that they don't accept controversial advertisements (Hiaasen 2004).

At least twenty-five organizations now give college scholarships to GLBT individuals, including The Point Foundation, Parents and Friends of Lesbians and Gays, The League at AT&T Foundation, and the United Church of Christ (Kahn 2004). The largest source of scholarships in 2004 was The Point Foundation, which funded twenty-seven individuals.

* * *

There's no doubt that things are much better for the GLBT community than they were several decades ago. Increasing numbers of people in the straight community are becoming allies to GLBT people or at least have a "live and let live" philosophy. In spite of this progress, the United States still has a long way to go to eliminate discrimination based on sexual orientation.

7

Social Change and Social Movements

HOW CAN WE ACHIEVE GREATER EQUALITY WHEN IT COMES TO issues of race, class, gender, and sexual orientation? The answer: more of us must participate in social change activities. According to one of the slogans of the 1960s, "If you are not part of the solution, you are part of the problem."

Beverly Tatum (2003) uses the analogy of a pedestrian conveyor belt at an airport. Being on the conveyor belt gives you an advantage over those walking beside it, whether you are taking steps or standing still. You must get off the belt or stop the belt to get rid of the unfair advantage. Similarly, members of dominant groups must take action to create more equality for subordinate groups. Doing nothing simply perpetuates the privilege of the dominant groups.

The next logical question is, What is to be done? There should be no surprise when I tell you that neither social scientists nor activists agree on the answer to this important question. Throughout this book I have emphasized the need to look at issues from different levels of analysis. This is also true of change.

▪ Action for Social Change

Levels of Action

There are at least three different levels of action with regard to change. The lowest level is to change yourself. To the extent that you hold prejudiced attitudes or buy into the dominant ideology, try to ask yourself whether this is what you really want to believe. One of my aims with this book was to make you aware of various forms of oppression and how you, if you are a member of the dominant group, may be perpetuating them. You may have already begun to examine some of your beliefs and to question others. You can also change your behavior if that is warranted. If you sometimes make racist, sexist, or homophobic remarks, you don't have to keep doing this. If you are a male who tends to treat women as sex objects, you can change. I hope that none of you participate in hate crimes, but if you do, stop! We all have the ability to change what we believe and how we act.

Although self-change is a good thing, it is not nearly enough. We live in a world with other people who have their own attitudes and behaviors. More importantly, we exist in a set of social, cultural, and economic institutions that are all part of the oppressions that we have been discussing. True change must go beyond changing oneself.

The other end of the levels-of-action spectrum is collective social action, which refers to joining together with others to seek institutional change. This could mean joining and becoming active in an informal group or a formal organization that is committed to change. The action could involve letter writing, lobbying, and voter registration. It could also involve protest marches, demonstrations, and rallies. Minimally, you could participate in some of these activities. Those more committed would help to *organize* these activities. This takes more time and effort than self-change activities.

Another form of collective social action is to become part of a social movement. According to Freeman and Johnson (1999, 3), a social movement refers to "the mobilization and organization of large numbers of people to pursue a common cause. It is also used for the community of believers that is created by that mobilization." Social movements usually contain many organizations that are willing to act on the same issue. A single organization that influences only its own members is not usually thought of as a social movement.

The goals of collective social actions are (1) to attract new members, (2) to educate those who are participating for the first time, and (3) to let decisionmakers know that there will be consequences for not doing what the activists advocate. The consequences could include being voted out of office, being faced with political disruptions around the country, being confronted by consumer boycotts, and being forced to spend more funds on security. In some cases, social movements can result in genuine revolutions where the nature of political and economic power is fundamentally changed. Strong, broad-based social movements are much more likely to result in institutional change than any kind of individual actions. "Research shows that social movements can affect government policy, as well as how it is made. And movement influence extends further. Activism often profoundly changes the activists, and through them, the organizations in which they participate, as well as the broader culture" (Meyer 2003, 31).

Somewhere in the space between the individual and the collective social action approaches to change lies a third approach: *the micropolitics of subtle transformation.* According to this approach,

> We are doing important social justice work when we stop someone at a party from telling a racist joke, when we build ways for people to express themselves in classrooms, [and] when we find ways to get institutions to serve the interests of members of groups that have been excluded. These sorts of actions can change social institutions when many people are doing them at the same time. They operate as subtle but persistent internal pressure. (Kaufman 2003, 296–297)

In this way, micropolitics can result in discussions and change actions at the individual level as well as lawsuits against individual employers, schools, and local governments. Cynthia Kaufman cautions that simply being nice to people isn't enough: "A kindness that stays within the boundaries of the social structures that continually reproduce themselves doesn't make much of a difference except to the people it touches. But when our small-scale challenges interrupt the reproduction of a system of oppression, then something more is happening" (2003, 298).

If one were interested in promoting gay rights, for example, the individual change approach would suggest that you understand and try to overcome whatever homophobia you have internalized over the years. The micropolitics approach would suggest that you object to homophobic remarks among your friends and coworkers. The collective social action approach would suggest that you help to organize and attend local and national gay rights demonstrations to promote gay marriage or to protest against violence against gays.

Political Philosophy

Change also depends on one's political and philosophic perspectives about how society is supposed to work. Although people often identify themselves as conservatives, liberals, or radicals, it is becoming more and more difficult to give concise descriptions of these terms (see Chapter 1).

Traditional conservatives tend to put their faith in the market forces of capitalism and favor limited government programs and regulations, especially at the federal level. In terms of race and gender discrimination, conservatives now reluctantly acknowledge that the federal government has a limited role to play by punishing individual perpetrators and compensating individual victims.

Traditional liberals are also pro-capitalist in that they believe in market forces, but they understand that an unrestrained economy can get itself into difficulty. Liberals, therefore, believe that some limited regulation of the economy by the federal government is a necessity, as are programs for the dispossessed. They also believe that the federal government has a legitimate role in passing laws and programs to improve equal opportunities for women and people of color.

Radicals tend to be anti-capitalist in that they see a market-oriented economy as part of the problem. They argue that liberals and conservatives simply have different ways of maintaining American capitalism and the race, class, gender, and sexual orientation inequalities that go along with it. They are likely to promote social movements for change. Unfortunately, radicals don't agree about what to replace capitalism with. Some argue for a centrally planned, democratically controlled, government-owned economy called socialism. Others believe that there should be a more mixed economy where publicly and privately owned institutions coexist. Some radicals emphasize race whereas others emphasize class, gender, or sexual orientation.

One way to look at how these different political perspectives might deal with a social problem is to consider educational inequality. It is well-known that both race and family income influence how much education children are likely to receive. Whites and Asians do better in school than blacks, Hispanics, and Native Americans. Students from higher-income families tend to do better than those from lower-income families. At the risk of oversimplification, let me explain how these different political perspectives might view policies for change.

The key conservative solution to this problem is school choice. Conservatives argue that since the public schools have a near-monopoly on education, there is no incentive for them to provide decent educations. If the public schools would have to compete for students with private and parochial schools by the use of vouchers for poor students, the public schools would have to improve or they would go out of business. Under the No Child Left Behind Act, poor parents, many of whom are blacks and Hispanics, would be able to take their children out of poorly performing public schools and send them to better-performing private and parochial schools. In other words, a more open educational marketplace is supposed to help improve the nation's schools and equalize educational opportunities.

Liberals, including the major teachers' unions, argue that government should provide more money to the public schools in order to improve the quality of teachers and educational materials. Higher salaries and better mentoring would improve the quality of teachers. Newer and better books, more computers, more effective pedagogy, and smaller classes would help students to learn. They argue that a special focus, including funding, must be placed on schools with large numbers of poor and minority students.

Radicals, while agreeing with many of the liberal policies, would argue that the schools provide upward mobility for the few and reproduce inequality for the many. In addition to teaching students the skills they need to succeed in the labor force, radical teachers work to transform the curriculum to help students understand the roots of their own oppression and introduce them to social movements that will lead to change. Teachers should see themselves as transformative intellectuals rather than socializers to the dominant culture.

Electoral Politics

In the United States, when most people think of political activism, they probably think of elections. I always vote, and I usually find myself voting for the Democratic Party candidate for the simple reason that he or she is the lesser of two evils. There has rarely been a major party candidate that I enthusiastically supported. During the 2004 presidential election, for example, I just couldn't bring myself to put a Kerry/Edwards sign on my front lawn even though I was strongly anti-Bush. I voted for Kerry/Edwards, but with little enthusiasm. The two-party political system in the United States restricts our choices and limits the nature of debate. It is often impossible for third parties to be heard.

Although this is not the place to debate the efficacy of electoral politics, I have not included mainstream electoral groups in the following list of activist organizations. In some cases, elections can be part of a program of collective social action. When Jesse Jackson ran for president in 1984 and 1988, his campaign was part of an attempt to build the Rainbow Coalition, which was to be an independent organization that would survive the election. The 1980 election of Harold Washington as mayor of

Chicago was another example of genuine grassroots mobilization. However, fundamental social change requires political action that goes above and beyond electoral politics (Zinn 2003).

Single- vs. Multiple-Category Approaches

Some individuals and organizations focus on change for single categories such as race or class, or gender or sexual orientation. They may focus on only one of these issues without dealing with any of the others. Women might focus on gender issues exclusively, or Asians might focus only on racial issues. Other groups may focus on more than one category, but they may see one category as the most fundamental with the others being of lesser importance. Marxists, for example, have traditionally seen class as the main axis of oppression, with race and gender being less important.

Intersectionality theorists argue that the four categories are so interconnected that change in one requires changes in the others. In dealing with poverty, for example, women of color are heavily overrepresented among the poor. Any attempt to organize the poor would mean considering all three categories at the same time.

This multiple-category approach can be confusing if proponents don't accurately connect the dots to explain how one type of oppression is connected with another. In addition, this approach can create tensions when not everyone accepts the connection. Gay males and lesbians, for example, say that laws that prevent them from marrying are a civil rights issue, not unlike the laws that discriminated against blacks during the Jim Crow era. Many blacks, especially those involved with Christian fundamentalist churches, strongly object to this attempt to equate the two types of oppression on moral grounds. Other black leaders, such as Julian Bond (chair of the NAACP) and Congressman John Lewis (D-Ga.), support gay marriage as a civil rights issue (Bean 2004).

My experience tells me that the majority of students feel most comfortable with liberal, single-category approaches to individual change and micropolitics. My own approach is to emphasize radical, multiple-category, collective social action. Since I have found that most students don't know very much about the important impact that collective social action, especially social movements, has had in the United States, I will spend the rest of the chapter discussing this. First, I will provide a brief history of social movements dealing with class, race, gender, and sexual orientation. Then I will discuss contemporary collective social action possibilities in the twenty-first century.

▦ The History of Collective Social Action

The United States has had a long history of collective social action in the fight for class, race, and gender equality.[1] Sometimes the action is carried out by individual organizations and their members. Other times the action rises to the level of being a social movement. Unfortunately, many history books do not emphasize the role of collective social action in achieving progressive change.

Before the Civil War

During the first half of the nineteenth century, a strong biracial antislavery movement developed. White abolitionists (e.g., William Lloyd Garrison, Elizabeth Cady Stanton, and John Brown) and black abolitionists (e.g., David Walker, Frederick Douglass, and Martin Delany) traveled the country calling for the end of slavery. Harriet Tubman and others helped thousands of slaves to escape through the Underground Railroad. In addition, more than 200 documented slave revolts occurred, the most famous of which was led by Nat Turner.

There were important contradictions within the abolitionist movement, however. Many abolitionists believed in genuine racial equality. Others believed that blacks were inferior to whites but disagreed with slavery as an institution. White and black women were an important part of the abolitionist movement, but they were also promoting women's rights. In her famous "Ain't I a Woman" speech in 1851, Sojourner Truth made the argument that black women were also women even though they didn't have the privileges that white women had. In the end, male abolitionists decided to put women's rights on the back burner until slavery was abolished.

The first convention to promote women's rights, including the right to vote, was held in Seneca Falls, New York, in 1848. Stanton and Lucretia Mott were the main organizers. It took seventy-two more years for the suffragist movement to win the right for women to vote when the states finally approved the Nineteenth Amendment to the Constitution in 1920. This came to be known as the "first wave" of the women's movement.

Civil War–World War I

After the post–Civil War period of Reconstruction came to an end, legal segregation was reimposed in the South in the 1880s and 1890s. The US

Supreme Court put its stamp of approval on legal segregation in the *Plessy v. Ferguson* decision in 1896. The Court declared that policies of "separate but equal" (which were actually separate and unequal) were consistent with the US Constitution.

The black community was politically mobilized to fight for equality in the late nineteenth and early twentieth centuries. W. E. B. DuBois and Booker T. Washington had a running debate during this period over the issue of Jim Crow (legal) segregation in the South. Whereas Washington argued that blacks should try to make the best of a bad situation, DuBois argued for integration and the end of segregation. He helped to found the Niagara Movement in 1909, which evolved into the National Association for the Advancement of Colored People (NAACP). Using the courts, the NAACP led a decades-long struggle against lynching, school segregation, and the lack of voting rights.

Workers began to organize trade unions in the late nineteenth century to combat the growing power of the owners of large corporations, including J. P. Morgan, John D. Rockefeller, Andrew Carnegie, James Mellon, Cornelius Vanderbilt, and Leland Stanford. These men were often referred to as "robber barons." Since workers didn't have the right to organize at that time, they had to fight against the private armies of the robber barons. This was class struggle in its most literal sense since strikes often involved violent actions on both sides. Gradually, some employers recognized unions, wages in some industries increased, and the length of the workday was reduced somewhat. Workers did not get the right to collective bargaining until 1935.

The labor movement had a mixed record when it came to dealing with black and women workers. The American Federation of Labor (AFL, founded in 1881) consisted mostly of white male skilled workers. At various times the AFL excluded blacks, women, and immigrants from Mexico, Japan, and China. The more radical International Workers of the World (founded in 1905) included everyone in its "One Big Union." The Congress of Industrial Organizations (CIO), which formed in 1935, also organized all workers. In some industries, blacks and women formed their own unions, including the Brotherhood of Sleeping Car Porters and the International Ladies Garment Workers Union.

Other radical groups were active in the late nineteenth and early twentieth centuries. The American Socialist Party (founded in 1901) had 100,000 members at the height of its influence. In 1911 there were more than 1,200 elected socialist officials in 340 municipalities. Eugene Debs ran for president of the United States on the Socialist Party ticket five times. In 1912 in the election eventually won by Woodrow Wilson, Debs received 900,000 votes, about 6 percent of the total vote. Although the Socialist Party included some blacks in its membership, it "did not go much out of its way to act on the race question" (Zinn 2003, 347).

World War I–Brown *Decision*

The Communist Party (CP) split off from the Socialist Party after World War I and was active during the Depression in an attempt to mobilize working people. The CP fought for stronger unions and more government services for the unemployed and fought against evictions when people couldn't afford to pay rent. It also actively recruited blacks and other people of color and campaigned against segregation and lynchings. The black author Richard Wright was a member for a period of time, and W. E. B. DuBois and Paul Robeson were publicly sympathetic to the CP.

The Wagner Act, passed in 1935, finally gave workers the right to collective bargaining. The National Labor Relations Board was to enforce worker rights. However, the act didn't cover domestic workers and agricultural workers, most of whom were people of color and/or women.

The federal government, including the military, remained segregated even under liberal president Franklin Delano Roosevelt. In 1941, A. Phillip Randolph, the head of the Brotherhood of Sleeping Car Porters, threatened to organize a march on Washington to protest discrimination, especially in defense industries. Faced with the possibility of 100,000 angry blacks in Washington, President Roosevelt signed Executive Order 8822, which created the Equal Employment Practices Committee and abolished race discrimination in the federal government and in defense industries. During World War II, blacks, who were still treated as second-class citizens, and Japanese, who were interned in US concentration camps, still enlisted in the armed forces. However, they fought in segregated units led by white officers. After the end of World War II, in 1948 President Harry Truman finally issued an executive order that banned race discrimination in the armed forces.

After many years of political struggle and legal battles, the US Supreme Court outlawed legal segregation in public education in the 1954 *Brown v. Board of Education* decision. This overturned the "separate but equal" doctrine of *Plessy v. Ferguson*. Although *Brown* established an important legal precedent, many southern politicians refused to implement it, so the rule of Jim Crow remained throughout much of the South until a powerful grassroots social movement challenged racism.

Brown *Decision–1960s*

The modern civil rights movement is usually said to have begun in 1955 with the boycott of public buses in Montgomery, Alabama. Buses then had a movable partition that blacks had to sit behind. When all the white seats were filled, the driver would move the partition and blacks would have to give their seats to whites. Rosa Parks, an NAACP activist, refused to move one day and was arrested. The black community boycotted the buses for 381 days until a federal court declared the Montgomery law unconstitutional. The Southern Christian Leadership Conference (SCLC) grew out of this boycott, and the young Martin Luther King Jr. came into national prominence.

The civil rights movement was largely based on a combination of Christian faith and the principles of nonviolence articulated by Mahatma Gandhi during the anti-British revolution in India. Through boycotts, sit-ins, freedom rides, marches, demonstrations, and various other kinds of civil disobedience, King hoped to embarrass the South before the rest of the country in order to promote federal civil rights legislation. Because of southern intransigence and the growing strength and militance of the civil rights movement, Presidents Eisenhower and Kennedy were forced to use federal troops to enforce the *Brown* decision on school desegregation throughout the South.

Since civil rights activists were largely integrationists in that they wanted black people to be accepted into the mainstream of American life as equals, they tried to project an image of middle-class respectability. Demonstrators often marched and went to jail dressed in their Sunday best. They were encouraged to be disciplined and nonviolent and to control their anger at the police, who often abused them. White allies, especially liberals and labor union members, were welcomed in civil rights protests and organizations.

By 1960, however, a parallel movement for black liberation began to develop. Increasing numbers of young black activists began to articulate the ideology of Black Power. Organizations like the Student Nonviolent Coordinating Committee (SNCC) and the Congress of Racial Equality (CORE) talked about black political and economic power as well as cultural pride in their African heritage. Blacks, they demanded, must be accepted and negotiated with as a group and on their own terms. Nonviolence was downgraded from a religious principle to a political tactic that was appropriate in some situations and not in others. Whites who were interested in civil rights were told to do their political work in the white community and in white organizations, not in the black community. In some cases, the tactics of the Black Power movement conflicted with those of the civil rights movement.

The famous March on Washington, wherein Martin Luther King gave his "I Have a Dream" speech, was held in 1963 to convince President Kennedy and the Congress to pass a federal civil rights act that was stalled in Congress. Two hundred thousand people attended the nonviolent demonstration. It took the assassination of President Kennedy to get the Civil Rights Act of 1964 passed by Congress and signed by President Lyndon Johnson, a southern Democrat. The following year, the Voting Rights Act was passed by Congress. A few days later, the predominantly black Watts section of Los Angeles exploded in violence. This was the first of many riots and urban insurrections that were to plague the country for the rest of the decade, especially after the assassination of King in 1968. American cities were literally going up in flames. According to Zinn (2003), the year 1967 saw eight major riots, thirty-three serious riots, and 125 minor incidents.

The Black Panther Party and the League of Revolutionary Black Workers were both black Marxist organizations that were explicitly anti-capitalist. The league did most of its organizing work in the automobile factories of Detroit and other midwestern cities, seeing its enemies as both the big three automobile corporations and the United Auto Workers Union. The Panthers, in comparison, tried to organize poor black communities in cities outside of the South. Both groups worked in coalition with predominantly white anti-capitalist groups.

The civil rights movement inspired Mexican and Filipino migrant farmworkers in California to form the United Farm Workers Union (UFW) under the leadership of Cesar Chavez, who was sometimes called the Mexican Martin Luther King. Since farmworkers were not covered under the National Labor Relations Act, they had to fight to get growers to recognize their union with no help from federal officials. The strike began in the grape fields in 1965 and later spread to the lettuce fields. Not having enough power to confront the growers at the local level, the UFW launched a national grape boycott in 1967, asking ordinary citizens throughout the country not to buy grapes grown in California. After three years, the growers finally gave in and negotiated contracts with the UFW. This organizing campaign would not have been successful without broad-based support for the grape boycott.

The civil rights and Black Power movements spawned several other important social movements in the early 1960s. Students for a Democratic Society (SDS), a predominantly white and middle-class group, fought for student rights and racial and economic equality on and off college campuses. SDS became more Marxist and anti-capitalist by the end of the 1960s and was an important force among young people. The Weather Underground split off from SDS and believed it was necessary to engage in armed struggle to achieve change. As students became older and graduated or became young faculty members, many joined the New University Conference (NUC), which was known as the "adult SDS."

The movement against the war in Vietnam was also a major force in the 1960s, especially after 1964. Since young men were being drafted into the armed forces, the war had a personal effect on many families. In addition to groups like SDS and NUC, there were several large coalitions that organized major demonstrations each year in Washington, New York, San Francisco, and/or Los Angeles. More than 500,000 people gathered at some demonstrations to protest the war. Most of the time the demonstrations were peaceful, but other times some of the demonstrators destroyed property that was symbolically linked to the war (e.g., a recruiting station) or to the capitalist class (e.g., a bank). SDS was one of the main organizers of the militant demonstrations and the resulting police riot at the Democratic National Convention in Chicago in 1968. The antiwar movement had become so strong that national leaders had to consider the potentially militant reaction by demonstrators when they talked about escalating the war in Vietnam.

Government officials were so concerned with the rising level of militance, especially in the black community, that the FBI launched a counterintelligence program in the late 1960s called COINTELPRO. The FBI spied on activist groups, tried to disrupt the planning of demonstrations, and worked to discredit movement leaders (like tapping the phone of Martin Luther King). Local police departments organized "red squads," which did the same thing on the local level. Due to violent attacks by the police and political repression by the courts, the Black Panthers were eliminated as an effective organization by the early 1970s.

The late 1960s also saw the early developments of the second wave of the women's liberation movement. In 1963, the President's Commission on the Status of Women issued a widely publicized report documenting the second-class status of women in and out of the labor force. That same year, Betty Friedan's *Feminine Mystique* (1963) raised a number of issues, including educated, middle-class women being unhappily confined in isolated nuclear families. In 1964, the word *sex* was inserted into the Civil Rights Act, thereby banning discrimination against working women. The EEOC, however, didn't enforce the sex provision and said that an NAACP-like organization for women was needed.

As a result the National Organization for Women (NOW) was founded in 1966. A predominantly white, middle-class organization, NOW began to raise issues such as childcare, sex-role socialization, reproductive rights, equal pay for equal work, women entering predominantly male jobs, and electing more women to political office. It unsuccessfully tried to gain passage of an Equal Rights Amendment to the US Constitution in the 1970s. This simple amendment stated, "Equality of rights under the law shall not be denied or abridged by the United States or by any State on account of sex" (Eisler and Hixson 2001, 424). The amendment was passed by Congress in 1972 but fell three states short of ratification.

Women around the country also began meeting in small "consciousness-raising groups" to discuss what was going on in their family, work, and political lives. By learning that what appeared to be personal, private problems were also shared by other women, thousands of women grew to understand the nature of patriarchy. One important slogan became "The personal is political." Whereas NOW represented mostly liberal feminists, these smaller groups fed into the radical feminist and socialist feminist wings of the women's movement.

The gay liberation movement came to national prominence in 1969 when gay males fought back after police raided the Stonewall bar in New York's Greenwich Village. However, two early gay rights organizations, the Mattachine Society and the Daughters of Bilitis, had been founded in the 1950s. After Stonewall, gay men and lesbians began coming out of the closet in large numbers and demanding their rights in the workplace, schools, and cultural institutions as well as freedom from police harassment (Esterberg 1996).

These movements had an impact on social change. The antiwar movement put restraints on how much military force could be used in Vietnam, and this contributed to the US withdrawal in 1973. The civil rights and Black Power movements, along with the urban rebellions, forced policymakers to think about how to address the issues in America's inner cities. The women's movement helped to produce a sea change in the relations between men and women as well as changes in the labor market. Unfortunately, many contemporary young women believe that a women's movement is no longer necessary.

One of the slogans that came out of the 1960s was "The people, united, can never be defeated." Although the different social movements were not always united with each other, they show that groups of people, acting together, can achieve meaningful institutional change. This lesson should not be lost in the twenty-first century.

▪ Contemporary Issues and Activism

Because a complete history of social activism in the United States is beyond the scope of this book, I'd like to fast-forward to the first decade of the twenty-first century. In spite of the increasingly conservative nature of the political times, there are still a variety of issues that are of interest to college-age young people, and there are a variety of organizations that address themselves to these issues. Toward the end of the semester, a handful of students usually ask me that big question: What can I do? In the last part of this chapter, I'd like to answer that question by discussing some of the main activist organizations that are working on the issues that have been discussed in previous chapters.

I've tried to limit this discussion to national organizations that have regional or local affiliates that readers can join and be active in. I have omitted many excellent organizations that only exist in one or two cities. Due to space limitations, I have also omitted organizations that provide excellent educational resources but that do not participate in activism themselves. Finally, most of the organizations have a liberal or radical political orientation. This reflects the reality that most conservatives are just not interested in promoting the rights of workers, people of color, women, and gays as separate groups either through activism or other means.

Workers' Rights

US workers face difficult times in the early twenty-first century. During the four years of the first Bush administration (2000–2004), there was a net loss of more than 1 million jobs from the United States, part of which has been caused by multinational corporations outsourcing some jobs and moving entire factories overseas because of cheaper labor. Computers and other labor-saving devices have also reduced jobs. Benefits and retirement pensions have been reduced, as have government transfer payments. The percentage of workers in labor unions has been declining for several decades, and, as a result, workers have less decisionmaking power than they did in the past.

Some unions are beginning to understand "that organizing and growth are linked to mobilizing outsiders in the new labor markets, including new-economy workers, people of color, women, and immigrant workers" (Ness 2003, 56). The Hotel Employees and Restaurant Employees Union (HERE) has been increasingly successful in organizing hotel workers around the country, especially in Las Vegas, Nevada. The

Service Employees International Union (SEIU) has successfully organized custodians and other building service workers. The United Needletrades, Industrial, and Textile Employees Union (UNITE) has organized industrial laundries. In order to increase their bargaining power, UNITE merged with HERE in 2004 to form UNITE HERE.

SEIU and UNITE HERE have been critical of the AFL-CIO leadership for spending too much time supporting Democratic Party political candidates and not enough resources increasing the number of workers that are in unions. In September 2005, these two unions, along with five others, broke away from the AFL-CIO and formed another national labor organization called Change to Win.

College students can support workers' rights in several ways. If workers on your campus are trying to organize a union, support them. They could be janitors, clerical workers, or teaching assistants. Join their picket lines and help pressure the administration to recognize the union and increase wages and benefits. Since many campus workers are people of color, immigrants, and women, union struggles involve more than just class issues.

United Students Against Sweatshops (USAS, www.studentsagainst sweatshops.org) often supports these struggles, although it mainly focuses on making sure that the licensed equipment sold by universities is not made in sweatshops either here or abroad. The term *sweatshop* usually refers to workplaces with long hours, low pay, and unsafe and/or unhealthy working conditions. With chapters at over 150 college campuses around the country, USAS has gotten many universities to adopt Campus Codes of Conduct, which include public disclosure of factory sites, independent monitoring of factory conditions, and guaranteed living wages for workers that produce the licensed equipment (Kelly and Lefkowitz 2003).

SweatshopWatch.org is another organization that tries to improve pay and working conditions in sweatshops around the world. According to the website, Sweatshop Watch was founded in 1995 and

> is a coalition of over 30 labor, community, civil rights, immigrant rights, women's, religious and student organizations, and many individuals, committed to eliminating the exploitation that occurs in sweatshops. Sweatshop Watch serves low-wage workers nationally and globally, with a focus on garment workers in California. We believe that workers should earn a living wage in a safe, decent work environment, and that those responsible for the exploitation of sweatshop workers must be held accountable.

Jobs With Justice (www.jwj.org) is a somewhat broader organization that "connect[s] labor, faith-based community, and student organizations to work together on workplace and community social justice campaigns." According to its website, JWJ has coalitions in forty cities throughout the country. Its Student Labor Action Project is geared specifically to high school and college students.

Some students may want to get training to become a union organizer. The Union Summer program (www.unionsummer.aflcio.org), begun by the AFL-CIO in 1996, has trained over 3,000 activists. It is a five-week, paid educational internship that includes a weeklong orientation and placement in various parts of the country.

Another summer experience is the Strategic Corporate Research Summer School (www.campaignforlaborrights.org/index/apr03/announce5_school.htm) at the Cornell University School of Industrial and Labor Relations. Graduate students and advanced undergraduates are exposed to a one-week course emphasizing "a comprehensive introduction to the nature and structure of corporate ownership, finance and power in today's economy." The goal is to provide students with research skills that can be helpful during union-organizing drives.

The AFL-CIO also has an Organizing Institute (www.organize.aflcio.org) that offers two programs. The 3-Day Training Program teaches the basic tactics and strategy used by the labor movement; housing and food are provided. The Field Training Program includes a two-week orientation and three months of field training wherein students work in an actual organizing campaign. The weekly stipend was $450 in 2004 plus housing, transportation, and health insurance. Successful trainees will be hired as union organizers.

The Asian-Pacific American Labor Alliance (www.aplanet.org), affiliated with the AFL-CIO, is a membership organization of Asian Pacific Union members. It sponsored the 2003 Immigrant Workers Freedom Ride, which toured the country to raise consciousness about the problems of immigrant workers. The "freedom ride" designation, of course, was taken from the freedom rides of the 1960s that protested segregated public transportation.

Finally, those interested in the concerns of women in the labor force should check out 9 to 5, National Association of Working Women (www.9to5.org). Founded in 1974, 9 to 5 is committed to improving the position of women in the paid labor force. It lobbies for legislation at the federal, state, and local levels to win family-friendly policies for low-wage women, including welfare reform and equal rights on the job. It also has a Job Survival Hotline to handle individual complaints.

Race

There are many organizations involved in protecting and enhancing the civil rights of specific race and ethnic groups. This includes issues concerning education, voting rights, employment, and government programs providing help for the disadvantaged. Typically, these groups are politically liberal and tend to focus on a specific race and/or ethnic category.

The oldest of the organizations is the nearly 100-year-old NAACP—the National Association for the Advancement of Colored People (www.naacp.org). Although it gained a somewhat "stodgy" reputation during the turbulent 1960s and 1970s, the NAACP has begun to recruit more young people in recent years and is one of the most well-known of the civil rights organizations in the black community. The National Urban League (www.nul.org) is another traditional civil rights organization.

Other race and ethnic groups also have this type of civil rights organization. The National Council of La Raza (www.nclr.org) is the umbrella group for the Hispanic community. The Asian community has the Organization of Chinese Americans (www.ocantl.org), the Organization of Japanese Americans (www.janet.org), and the Japanese American Citizens League (www.jacl.org). American Indians don't have a national organization that individuals can join at the local level; the closest to that would be the National Congress of American Indians (www.ncai.org), a tribal membership organization. The National Network for Immigrant and Refugee Rights (www.nnirr.org) handles issues regarding immigrants of all races.

The civil rights organizations of Arab Americans and Muslims have become especially important since September 11. They include the Arab-American Anti-Discrimination Committee (www.adc.org) and the Council on American-Islamic Relations (www.CAIR-net.org). The Tikkun Community (www.tikkun.org) is a predominantly Jewish group that supports Arab and Muslim rights in both the United States and the Middle East.

In addition to these civil rights organizations, there are other race-related groups that go beyond civil rights. The Black Radical Congress (www.blackradicalcongress.org), for example, is a more left-leaning group that calls for large-scale social change. As its website states, "Recognizing the contributions from diverse tendencies within Black Radicalism—including socialism, revolutionary nationalism and feminism—we are united in opposition to all forms of oppression, including class exploitation, racism, patriarchy, homophobia, anti-immigration prejudice and imperialism." This is a relatively new group that formed in 1998.

Critical Resistance (www.criticalresistance.org), another left-leaning group, focuses on prisons where there is a huge overrepresentation of blacks and Hispanics. According to its website, "Critical Resistance seeks to build an international movement to end the Prison Industrial Complex by challenging the belief that caging and controlling people makes us safe. . . . As such, our work is part of global struggles against inequality and powerlessness."

The Anti-Defamation League (www.adl.org) is a more mainstream group that does excellent work monitoring a broad range of right-wing hate groups like the Aryan Nation and the various formations of the Ku Klux Klan. In addition to being explicitly racist, these predominantly white hate groups promote a vicious form of anti-Semitism.

Gender

There are a wide variety of national women's organizations with local chapters. The largest is the National Organization for Women (NOW), which was founded in 1966 (www.now.org). NOW claims 500,000 contributing members and 550 chapters in all fifty states and Washington, D.C. The organization is involved in a large variety of issues, including employment discrimination, reproductive rights, education, childcare, health, politics, and peace. The Feminist Majority (www.feminist.org) is another multi-issue organization, and it has an affiliated student organization called Feminist Campus (www.feministcampus.org).

Several women's organizations focus primarily on reproductive rights. Planned Parenthood (www.plannedparenthood.org) is primarily a service provider where women can get birth control counseling, gynecological exams, and abortions. NARAL Pro-Choice (www.naral.org) is an activist organization that fights for reproductive rights in terms of national and state legislation and court decisions. All four of these organizations were among the many cosponsors of the large national reproductive rights demonstrations that have been held during the past several years.

INCITE! Women of Color Against Violence (www.incite-national.org) works against all forms of violence against women. As stated on its website, the organization's goal is to "advance a national movement to nurture the health and well-being of communities of color." The National Organization for Men Against Sexism (www.nomas.org) is also dedicated to stopping violence against women and to promoting gender equality.

Finally, there are a number of women's organizations whose mission is to achieve peace and justice around the world and in the United States. The Women's International League for Peace and Freedom (www.wilpf.org) was founded in 1915 by Jane Addams of Hull House fame. Women's Actions for New Directions (www.wand.org) was founded in 1982 as Women's Action for Nuclear Disarmament. Women in Black (www.womeninblack.org) is an international organization that was founded in 1988 by Israeli women who called for a just peace between Israelis and Palestinians. Women in Black still focuses on the Middle East but is also involved in other international issues. Code Pink: Women for Peace (www.codepink4peace.org) is a much newer organization that was founded in 2002 as part of the movement against the war in Iraq. All of these organizations have participated in the various demonstrations against the war in Iraq.

Gay Rights

As discussed in the previous chapter, a lot of work remains to be done in order to achieve equality for the GLBT population. There are civil rights and legal issues with regard to employment, housing, education, healthcare, marriage, and domestic partnerships. In addition, AIDS prevention and treatment is a major issue, especially for gay men and for heterosexual women of color.

There are two national civil rights organizations with local chapters for the GLBT community. The Human Rights Campaign (HRC, www.hrc.org) website describes it as "a bipartisan organization that works to advance equality based on sexual orientation and gender expression and identity, to ensure that gay, lesbian, bisexual and transgender Americans can be open, honest and safe at home, at work and in the community." The HRC lobbies Congress, provides campaign support for gay-friendly candidates, and conducts public education campaigns. It has recently established Partnerships for Equality, which provides funds to state advocacy organizations to promote gay-friendly legislation.

The National Gay and Lesbian Task Force (NGLTF, www.thetaskforce.org) has a similar mission with a somewhat more activist orientation. According to its website, "We're building a social justice movement that unites ideas with action. We organize activists. We train leaders. We equip organizers. We mobilize voters. We build coalitions. We teach-and-learn from today's vibrant GLBT youth movement. We're proud of our commitment to the linkages between oppressions based on race, class, gender and sexual orientation." The NGLTF also has a think tank (The Policy Institute), tracks state legislation, and promotes local organizing through the Federation of Statewide Lesbian, Gay, Bisexual, and Transgender Political Organizations. Soulforce (www.soulforce.org) is another gay activist organization.

These websites are strangely silent around the issue of AIDS. The New York–based Gay Men's Health Crisis (www.gmhc.org) has a national orientation when it comes to education, but its treatment and policy orientation are focused only on New York. The only national organization with local chapters that deals with AIDS is ACT UP (www.actupny.org). ACT UP is really a loose network of groups that began in New York City and has spread to a dozen other cities. According to the website of the New York ACT UP chapter,

> We are a coalition of diverse individuals united in anger and committed to direct action to end the AIDS crisis. ACT UP is not a gay rights group. While the AIDS crisis is inextricably linked to homophobia (along with other modes of oppression) and a large number of our members come from the lesbian/gay/bi/trans communities, ACT UP is about fighting AIDS. Often this works in conjunction with queer liberation, but our primary focus is the fight against AIDS.

Tactically, ACT UP is more militant than most other groups in that it advocates direct action and civil disobedience to get its point across. Members have disrupted professional conferences and political meetings, and civil disobedience manuals are offered on the ACT UP website. In one of its early actions in 1993, ACT UP members dumped the ashes of friends and loved ones who died of AIDS on the steps of the California state capitol to protest cuts in healthcare spending (Shepard 2003). As part of the street protests at the Republican National Convention in 2004, ACT UP members took their clothes off and were arrested.

ACT UP also recognizes the global nature of AIDS. In 1999, the organization criticized then–vice president Al Gore for protecting the rights of multinational pharmaceutical corporations to charge high prices for their drugs in Third World countries. South Africa wanted to produce its own low-cost generic version of these expensive drugs to distribute to its predominantly poor population, where AIDS is transmitted primarily through heterosexual contact. Gore eventually backed down. According to ACT UP activist Vito Russo, "After we kick the shit out of this disease,

I intend to be able to kick the shit out of this system, so that this never happens again" (Shepard 2003, 153). Russo was referring to the fact that "fighting the AIDS pandemic [means] fighting institutional racism, sexism [and] the class system as well as homophobia" (Shepard 2003, 153).

Straight people who want to be supportive of GLBT friends and relatives can join Parents, Families, and Friends of Lesbians and Gays (PFLAG, www.pflag.org). With more than 500 affiliates throughout the country, PFLAG engages in a number of activities, including "education, to enlighten an ill-informed public; and advocacy, to end discrimination and to secure equal civil rights." It also provides opportunities to "dialogue" about a variety of issues around sexual orientation. The Gay, Lesbian, and Straight Education Network (www.glsen.org) focuses on safety in the schools for gay students.

Finally, Freedom to Marry (www.freedomtomarry.org) focuses on the issue of gay marriage. Log Cabin Republicans (online.logcabin.org) is a conservative organization that supports gay marriage and a variety of other gay issues.

Peace and Justice

A number of organizations focus on war and militarism; the current focus is on the US war against Iraq, which began in March 2003. In addition to questions concerning the immorality of the war and the critique of American militarism, the war in Iraq has implications for some of the issues discussed in previous chapters. First, the huge expense of the war makes it more difficult to fund a wide variety of social programs geared toward poor and working people, including whites and people of color. According to the Institute for Policy Studies (2005), the total cost of the war through August 31, 2005, was $204.4 billion, about $727 for each US citizen. This could have paid for 1.8 million affordable housing units or 40 million scholarships for college students or 27 million Head Start slots for a single year.

Second, people of color and low-income people are heavily overrepresented among soldiers fighting in Iraq and, therefore, are also overrepresented among the dead and wounded. For those at the lower income levels, the military is often seen as the best and least expensive way to get job training and pay for college. Although there is no legal draft at the time of this writing, there is a type of economic draft for low-income Americans.

The United States invaded Iraq on March 19, 2003, without the support of the United Nations or most of the world's countries. During the first Gulf War, in 1991, the United States, with the support of the United Nations, invaded Iraq to prevent Saddam Hussein from taking control of neighboring Kuwait. The main rationale for the 2003 invasion was that Iraq was an imminent threat to the security of the United States. The Bush administration insisted that Iraq (1) possessed weapons of mass destruction, and (2) had ties to al Qaida, the organization that engineered the September 11, 2001, attacks on the World Trade Center and the Pentagon.

Less than two months after the United States invaded Iraq, President Bush announced on May 1, 2003, that major hostilities had ended and that the United States was in control of Iraq. Despite that announcement, the Iraqis did not welcome American troops with open arms, and the violence and killing did not stop as a result of the US occupation of Iraq. By August 31, 2005, 1,882 US soldiers had been killed and over 14,000 had been wounded. Almost 3,000 Iraqi police and government soldiers and between 23,000 and 100,000 Iraqi civilians had also been killed. Finally, between 16,000 and 40,000 Iraqi resistance fighters had also been killed (Institute for Policy Studies 2005). The number of American dead topped 2,000 on October 25, 2005 (Boudreaux et al. 2005).

Subsequent events have undermined the Bush administration's justification for the invasion. Numerous reports have indicated that Iraq had no weapons of mass destruction and no ties to al Qaida at the time of the invasion. Hence, Saddam Hussein was not an immediate threat to the United States. The Abu Ghraib prison scandal of 2004, the continuing American occupation of Iraq, and the continuing US war in Afghanistan have further inflamed passions of the people of Iraq and Muslims all over the world.

The movement to oppose the war in Iraq began before the invasion. There was a national demonstration on October 26, 2002, and international demonstrations on January 18, 2003. After the invasion, the protests continued. Over 100,000 people protested the war on October 25, 2003. Between 400,000 and 500,000 marched outside the Republican National Convention on August 29, 2004.

Two national groups organize these large-scale national demonstrations and are active in local communities: International A.N.S.W.E.R. Coalition (Act Now to Stop War and End Racism; www.international ANSWER.org) and United for Peace and Justice (www.unitedforpeace. org). In addition to opposing the war, coalition members support the rights of women and people of color in the United States. The websites of both groups list hundreds of local activist organizations. The American Friends Service Committee (www.afsc.org), a pacifist Quaker organization, and Not in Our Name (www.notinourname.net) also participate in antiwar activities and have local offices throughout the country. Amnesty International (www.amnestyusa.org) focuses on human rights around the world.

Although it was formed in 1998, MoveOn (www.moveon.org) really took off in 2002 with online petitions and calls for activism. In 2004, MoveOn organized a serious of house parties in concert with the opening of Michael Moore's film *Fahrenheit 911*. After typing in your zip code on the MoveOn website, you would click on a home near you to reserve a seat. People then gathered in small groups to discuss the film and participate in a national conference call with Moore. A few months later, this same process was repeated with the showing of *Outfoxed*, a blistering critique of the conservative bias of the Fox News Network. These house parties have a huge potential to mobilize people at the local level.

Left-Wing Political Formations

Several organizations are working to build a socialist, rather than a capitalist, society. The Democratic Socialists of America (DSA, www.dsausa.org) is explicitly anti-capitalist but does not want to repeat the authoritarian errors of countries like the former Soviet Union. They are calling for a democratic form of socialism wherein the government would own a greater portion of the economy and ordinary people would have a much larger say in political decisions than they now have. The Committees of Correspondence for Democracy and Socialism (www.cc-ds.org) is also working for a socialist transformation. Neither of these groups runs candidates for political office; the DSA sees itself as trying to push the Democratic Party to the left.

The Green Party of the United States (www.gp.org), in contrast, does field candidates and sees itself as a third political party. Focusing on "environmentalism, non-violence, social justice, and grassroots organizing," Green Party candidates have participated in federal, state, and local political races since 1996. In the 2004 election, Green Party presidential candidate David Keith Cobb received less than 1 percent of the popular vote, but 221 Green Party members hold elected office in twenty-seven states.

Other Activist Groups

ACORN, the Association of Community Organizations for Reform Now (www.acorn.org), was founded in 1970 and claims 750 chapters in low-income neighborhoods throughout the country. It focuses on grass-roots community organizing for better housing, a living wage for low-income workers, more community investment from banks and government agencies, and better schools. Member tactics include "direct action, negotiation, legislation, and voter participation." The Industrial Areas Foundation (www.industrialareasfoundation.org) focuses on similar issues.

Independent Media Centers (www.indymedia.org) describes itself as "a network of collectively run media outlets for the creation of radical, accurate, and passionate tellings of the truth." The web-based organization arose in 1999 in conjunction with the Seattle, Washington, anti-globalization protests by broadcasting real-time coverage of the demonstrations. Local outlets generally invite articles from radical writers on a variety of topics and have calendars of local events and demonstrations. They are one of the few media sources where one can learn what happened at local demonstrations, since mainstream media frequently ignore these protests.

Another outlet for people who are interested in writing and research that can lead to activism is the US Public Interest Research Group (USPIRG, uspirg.org). Its mission is to "deliver persistent, result-oriented public interest activism that protects our environment, encourages a fair sustainable economy, and fosters responsive democratic government." USPIRG projects involve corporate reform, student aid, right-to-know rules, and a variety of environmental concerns, including Arctic drilling, clean air and water, and power plants.

*   *   *

As this chapter shows, there are numerous ways to become an activist to achieve a more just world. Many of these national organizations have chapters or affiliates in your city, possibly even on your campus. There are also thousands of local organizations that are working on the issues raised in these pages. Get involved! Remember, if you are not part of the solution, you are probably part of the problem.

▓ Note

1. This section was compiled from a number of sources, especially Takaki (1993) and Zinn (2003).

Key Terms

Bisexual refers to individuals who are sexually, physically, and emotionally attracted to both same- and opposite-sex partners.

Classism is a system that stigmatizes poor and working-class people and their cultures and assigns high status to the affluent and their culture solely because of their relative wealth.

Coming out refers to someone who has revealed his or her GLBT sexual orientation to others.

Conflict diversity refers to understanding how different groups exist in a hierarchy of inequality in terms of power, privilege, and wealth.

Counting diversity refers to empirically enumerating differences within a given population.

Culture diversity refers to the importance of understanding and appreciating the cultural differences between groups.

Discrimination refers to actions that deny equal treatment to persons perceived to be members of some social category or group.

A **dominant group** is a social group that controls the political, economic, and cultural institutions in a society.

The **essentialist** perspective argues that reality exists independent of our perception of it; that is, that there are real and important (essential) differences among categories of people.

An **ethnic group** is a social group that has certain cultural characteristics that set it off from other groups and whose members see themselves as having a common past.

Ethnoviolence refers to acts motivated by prejudice intending to do physical or psychological harm because of the victims' group membership.

Exploitation means that the dominant group uses the subordinate group for its own ends, including economic profit and higher position in the social hierarchy.

Feminism is a movement to end male supremacy.

Gay usually refers to homosexual males, although it is also used as an umbrella term for homosexuals in general.

Gender refers to the behavior that is culturally defined as appropriate and inappropriate for males and females.

GLBT stands for gay, lesbian, bisexual, and transgendered people.

Good-for-business diversity refers to the argument that businesses will be more profitable, and government agencies and not-for-profit corporations will be more efficient, with diverse labor forces.

Hegemonic ideologies are those ideas that are so influential that they dominate all other ideologies.

Heterosexism refers to a system of oppression against the GLBT population.

Heterosexual refers to persons who are sexually, physically, and emotionally attracted to people of the opposite sex.

Homophobia refers to the fear and hatred of those who love and sexually desire people of the same sex.

Homosexual refers to persons who are sexually, physically, and emotionally attracted to people of the same sex.

Ideology is a body of ideas reflecting the social needs and aspirations of an individual group, class, or culture.

Income is the amount of money that a family earns from wages and salaries, interest, dividends, rent, gifts, and transfer payments.

Individual discrimination refers to the behavior of individual members of one group/category that is intended to have a differential and/or harmful effect on members of another group/category.

Institutional discrimination refers to the policies of dominant group institutions, and the behavior of individuals who implement these policies and control these institutions, that are intended to have a differential and/or harmful effect on subordinate groups.

Intergenerational mobility is a child's class position relative to the child's parents.

In the closet refers to someone who has not revealed his or her GLBT sexual orientation to others.

Intersexed refers to a person having physical attributes of both males and females.

Intragenerational mobility is the degree to which a young worker who enters the labor force can improve his or her class position within a single lifetime.

Lesbian refers to homosexual females.

A **master status** is one that has a profound effect on one's life and that dominates or overwhelms the other statuses one occupies.

Meritocracy is a stratified society wherein the most skilled people have the better jobs and the least skilled people have the lowest-paying jobs, regardless of race, gender, age, and so on.

Occupational sex segregation refers to the differential distribution of men and women into sex-appropriate occupations in the labor force.

Oppression is a dynamic process by which one segment of society achieves power and privilege through the control and exploitation of other groups, which are burdened and pushed down into the lower levels of the social order.

The other is viewed as being unlike the dominant group in profoundly different, usually negative ways.

Passing refers to a subordinate-group member who successfully pretends to be a dominant-group member.

Patriarchy is a hierarchical system that promotes male supremacy.

Politics refers to any collective action that is intended to support, influence, or change social policy or social structures.

Prejudice refers to negative attitudes toward a specific group of people.

Privilege means that some groups have something of value that is denied to others simply because of the groups they belong to; these unearned advantages give some groups a head start in seeking a better life.

A **racial group** is a social group that is socially defined as having certain biological characteristics that set it apart from other groups, often in invidious ways.

Racial ideology is the racially based framework used by actors to explain and justify (dominant race) or challenge (subordinate race or races) the racial status quo.

Racism is a system of oppression based on race.

Role specifies expected behavior that goes along with a specific status.

Sex refers to the physical and biological differences between the categories of male and female.

Sexism is a system of oppression based on gender.

Sexual behavior refers to whom we have sex with.

Sexual identification refers to what people call themselves.

Sexual orientation is determined by to whom we are attracted sexually, physically, and emotionally.

The **social constructionist** perspective argues that reality cannot be separated from the way a culture makes sense of it—that meaning is "constructed" through social, political, legal, scientific, and other processes.

Social mobility refers to individuals moving up or down in terms of their class level.

Status refers to a position that one holds or a category that one occupies in a society.

Stereotypes are cultural beliefs about a particular group that are usually highly exaggerated and distorted, even though they may have a grain of truth.

Stigma is an attribute for which someone is considered bad, unworthy, or deeply discredited because of the category that he or she belongs to.

Straight refers to heterosexual people.

Stratification refers to the way in which societies are marked by inequality, by differences among people that are regarded as being higher or lower.

Structural discrimination refers to policies of dominant-group institutions, and the behavior of the individuals who implement these policies and control these institutions, that are race-/class-/gender-/sexuality-neutral in intent but that have a differential and/or harmful effect on subordinate groups.

A **subordinate group** is a social group that lacks control of the political, economic, and cultural institutions in a society.

Transgendered people feel that their gender identity doesn't match their physiological body.

Transsexuals are people who have had sex change operations.

Transvestites are people who like to cross-dress, that is, wear clothes that are culturally appropriate to the opposite sex.

Wealth refers to the assets that people own and is often expressed in terms of net worth.

Bibliography

Adams, J. Q., and Peaarlie Strother-Adams. 2001. *Dealing with Diversity.* Dubuque, Iowa: Kendall-Hunt.

Adams, Maurianne, Warren J. Blumenfeld, Rosie Castaneda, Heather W. Hackman, Madeline L. Peters, and Ximena Zuniga, eds. 2000. *Readings for Diversity and Social Justice: An Anthology on Racism, Antisemitism, Sexism, Heterosexism, Ableism, and Classism.* New York: Routledge.

Akom, A. A. 2000. "The House That Race Built: Some Observations on the Use of the Word *Nigga*, Popular Culture, and Urban Adolescent Behavior." In Lois Weis and Michelle Fine (eds.), *Construction Sites: Excavating Race, Class, and Gender Among Urban Youth.* New York: Teachers College Press.

Albert, Judith Clavira, and Steward Edward Albert. 1984. *The Sixties Papers: Documents of a Rebellious Decade.* New York: Praeger.

Allegretto, Sylvia, and Michelle M. Arthur. 2001. "An Empirical Analysis of Homosexual/Heterosexual Male Earnings Differentials: Unmarried and Unequal?" *Industrial and Labor Relations Review* 54, no. 3 (April): 631–646.

Allport, Gordon W. 1954. *The Nature of Prejudice.* Cambridge, Mass.: Addison Wesley.

Alonso-Zaldivar, Ricardo, and Jennifer Oldham. 2002. "New Airport Screener Jobs Going Mostly to Whites." *Los Angeles Times*, September 25. http://www.latimes.com.

Altemeyer, Bob. 2001. "Changes in Attitudes Toward Homosexuals." *Journal of Homosexuality* 42, no. 2: 63–75.

American-Arab Anti-Discrimination Committee. 2002. "Facts About Arabs and the Arab World." http://www.adc.org/index.php?id=248.

American Association of Retired People. 2004. "Civil Rights and Race Relations." www.aarp.org/research/reference/publicopinions/aresearch-import-854.html.

Anderson, Margaret L. 2003. *Thinking About Women: Sociological Perspectives on Sex and Gender.* Boston: Allyn and Bacon.

Anderson, Margaret L., and Patricia Hill Collins, eds. 2004. *Race, Class, and Gender: An Anthology.* 5th ed. Belmont, Calif.: Wadsworth.

Armstrong, David, and Peter Newcomb. 2004. "The Forbes 400." *Forbes* 174, no. 7 (October 11): 103–278.

Associated Press. 2004. "Texas Texts Won't Have 'Married Partners.'" *Baltimore Sun,* November 6: 5A.

———. 2003. "DeShawn Might Be Less Employable Than Cody, Research Shows." *Baltimore Sun,* September 28: 4A.

Babcock, Linda, and Sara Laschever. 2003. *Women Don't Ask: Negotiation and the Gender Divide.* Princeton, N.J.: Princeton University Press.

Badgett, M. V. Lee. 2000. "The Myth of Gay and Lesbian Affluence." *Gay and Lesbian Review Worldwide* 7, no. 2 (Spring): 22–26.

Baird, Venessa. 2001. *The No-Nonsense Guide to Sexual Diversity.* London: Verso.

Baltimore Sun. 2004. "Military Discharged 770 in '03 for Homosexuality." *Baltimore Sun,* June 21: 6A.

Banks, James A. 1994. *An Introduction to Multicultural Education.* Boston: Allyn and Bacon.

Battle, Juan, Natalie Bennett, and Todd C. Shaw. 2004. "From the Closet to a Place at the Table: Past, Present, and Future Assessments of Social Science Research on African American Gay, Bisexual, and Transgender Populations." *African American Research Perspectives* 10 (Spring/Summer): 9–26.

Battle, Juan, Cathy J. Cohen, Dorian Warren, Gerard Fergerson, and Suzette Audam. 2002. *Say It Loud, I'm Black and I'm Proud: Black Pride Survey 2000.* New York: Policy Institute of the National Gay and Lesbian Task Force.

Bean, Linda. 2004. "Are Civil-Rights Leaders Afraid of Same-Sex Marriage?" *DiversityInc,* February 6. http://www.diversityinc.com.

Beeghley, Leonard. 2005. *The Structure of Social Stratification in the United States.* 4th ed. Boston: Allyn and Bacon.

Bendick, Marc, Jr., Charles W. Jackson, and Victor A. Reinoso. 1994. "Measuring Employment Discrimination Through Controlled Experiment." *Review of Black Political Economy* (Summer): 24–48.

Berg, John C., ed. 2003. *Teamsters and Turtles? US Progressive Political Movements in the 21st Century.* Lanham, Md.: Rowman and Littlefield.

Blauner, Bob. 2001. *Still the Big News: Racial Oppression in America.* Philadelphia: Temple University Press.

———. 1992. "Talking Past Each Other: Black and White Languages of Race." *American Prospect* 10 (Spring): 55–64.

Blauner, Robert. 1972. *Racial Oppression in America.* New York: Harper and Row.

Blumenfeld, Warren J., and Diane Raymond. 2000. "Prejudice and Discrimination." In Maurianne Adams et al. (eds.), *Readings for Diversity and Social Justice.* New York: Routledge.

Bonilla-Silva, Eduardo. 2003. *Racism Without Racists: Color-Blind Racism and the Persistence of Racial Inequality in the United States.* Lanham, Md.: Rowman and Littlefield.

———. 2001. *White Supremacy and Racism in the Post–Civil Rights Era.* Boulder: Lynne Rienner.

Boudreaux, Richard, Louise Roug, Doug Smith, and P. J. Huffstutter. 2005. "2000th Death Spotlights Insurgents' Persistence, Lethal Roadside Bombs." *Baltimore Sun,* August 26: 1A, 11A.

Bowman, Karlyn H. 2004. "Attitudes About Homosexuality and Gay Marriage." *American Enterprise Institute Studies in Public Opinion.* http://www.aei.org.

Boylan, Jennifer Finney. 2003. *She's Not There: A Life in Two Genders.* New York: Broadway.

Browning, Lynnley. 2003. "US Income Gap Widening, Study Says." *New York Times,* September 23. http://www.nytimes.com/2003/09/25/business/25POOR.html.

Bureau of Labor Statistics. 2002. "Displaced Workers Summary." US Department of Labor. http://stats.bls.gov/news.release/disp.nr0.htm.

Campbell, Bernadette, E. Glenn Schellenberg, and Charlene Y. Senn. 1997. "Evaluating Measures of Contemporary Sexism." *Psychology of Women Quarterly* 21: 89–102.

Carr-Ruffino, Norma. 2003. *Managing Diversity: People Skills for a Multicultural Workplace.* 6th ed. Boston: Pearson.

Chronicle of Higher Education. 2004. "Educational Attainment of the US Population by Racial and Ethnic Group, 2003." *CHE Almanac Issue 2004–2005,* 51, no. 1 (August 27): 18.

Cole, Yoji. 2004. "For $50M + Diversity Plan, Abercrombie and Fitch Makes Racism Suit Go Away." *DiversityInc,* October 17. http://www.diversityinc.com/members/10331print.cfm.

Cyrus, Virginia. 2000. *Experiencing Race, Class, and Gender in the United States.* 3rd ed. Mountain View, Calif.: Mayfield.

Dang, Alain, and Somjen Frazier. 2004. "Black and Same-Sex Households in the United States: A Report from the 2000 Census." New York: National Gay and Lesbian Task Force Policy Institute and the National Black Justice Coalition. http://www.thetaskforce.org.

D'Arcy, Janice. 2005. "Religious Houses Stand Divided on Gay Marriage Debate." *Baltimore Sun,* January 30: 1A, 6A.

Davis, Riccardo A. 2004. "Rating Best and Worst Companies for GLBT Workers—New HRC Data." *DiversityInc,* September 29. http://www.diversityinc.com.

Detroit Free Press. 2001. "100 Questions and Answers About Arab Americans: A Journalist's Guide." http://www.freep.com/jobspage/arabs/arab1.html.

Dill, Bonnie Thornton, and Maxine Baca Zinn, eds. 1994. *Women of Color in US Society.* Philadelphia: Temple University Press.

DiversityInc. 2004. "DiversityInc's Top 50 Companies for Diversity 2004." *DiversityInc* 13 (June/July): 46–114.

DiversityInc Staff and Associated Press. 2004. "Cracker Barrel Racial-Bias Case Settled: Company OKs Training, Undercover Probes." *DiversityInc,* May 12. http://www.diversityinc.com/members/6806print.cfm.

Diversity News. 2004a. "Ex–Merrill Lynch Broker Wins $2.2M in Gender Bias Lawsuit." *DiversityInc,* April 21. http://www.diversityinc.com/public/ 6730print.cfm.

———. 2004b. "Gay Discrimination Policy Decision Chided." *DiversityInc,* May 12. http://www.diversityinc.com/public/6641.cfm.

———. 2004c. "Evangelist Apologizes for Anti-Gay Remark." *DiversityInc,* September 24. http://www.diversityinc.com/public/8737_2.cfm.

———. 2004d. "Printing Giant Ends Race-Bias Lawsuit with $15 Million." *DiversityInc,* October 25. http://www.diversityinc.com/public/9816print.cfm.

———. 2004e. "Third Airline Settles Discrimination Charges." *DiversityInc,* May 12. http://www.diversityinc.com/public/6655print.cfm.

D'Souza, Dinesh. 1999. "The Billionaire Next Door." *Forbes.* http://www.forbes. com/Forbes/99/1011/6409050a.htm.

DuBois, W. E. B. 1990. *The Souls of Black Folk.* New York: Vintage.

Economic Policy Institute. 2003. "Racial Discrimination Continues to Play a Part in Hiring Decisions." http://www.epinet.org/content.cfm/webfeatures_ snapshots.

Economist. 2004. "Ever Higher Society, Ever Harder to Ascend." http://www. economist.com/world/na/PrinterFriendly.cfm?Story_ID.

Edwards, Cliff. 2003. "Coming Out in Corporate America: Gays Are Making Huge Strides Everywhere but in the Executive Suite." *Business Week,* December 15: 64–72.

Ehrenreich, Barbara. 2001. *Nickel and Dimed: On (Not) Getting By in America.* New York: Metropolitan.

Ehrlich, Howard J. 1999. "Campus Ethnoviolence." In Fred L. Pincus and Howard J. Ehrlich (eds.), *Race and Ethnic Conflict: Contending Views on Prejudice, Discrimination, and Ethnoviolence.* Boulder: Westview.

Ehrlich, Howard J., Fred L. Pincus, and Deborah Lacy. 1997. *Intergroup Relations on Campus: UMBC, the Second Study.* Baltimore: Prejudice Institute.

Eisenstein, Zillah. 2004. "Sexual Humiliation, Gender Confusion, and the Horrors at Abu Ghraib." http://www.portside.edu.

Eisler, Riane, and Allie C. Hixson. 2001. "The Equal Rights Amendment: What Is It, Why Do We Need It, and Why Don't We Have It Yet?" In Shelia Ruth (ed.), *Issues in Feminism: An Introduction to Women's Studies.* Mountain View, Calif.: Mayfield.

Ellis, Lee. 1996. "Theories of Homosexuality." In Ritch C. Savin-Williams and Kenneth M. Cohen (eds.), *The Lives of Lesbians, Gays, and Bisexuals: Children to Adults.* Fort Worth: Harcourt Brace.

Equal Employment Opportunity Commission. 2004a. "Race-Based Charges: FY1992–2003." wysiwyg://main.1018/http://www.eeoc.gov/stats/race. html.

———. 2004b. "Sex-Based Charges: FY1992–2003." wysiwyg:http://www. eeoc.gov/stats/sex.html.

————. 2004c. "Sexual Harassment Charges." wysiwyg:http://www.eeoc.gov/stats/harass.html.

Espiritu, Yen Le. 1992. *Asian-American Panethnicity: Bridging Institutions and Identities.* Philadelphia: Temple University Press.

Esterberg, Kristin Gay. 1996. "Gay Cultures, Gay Communities: The Social Organization of Lesbians, Gay Men, and Bisexuals." In Ritch C. Savin-Williams and Kenneth M. Cohen (eds.), *The Lives of Lesbians, Gays, and Bisexuals: Children to Adults.* Fort Worth: Harcourt Brace.

Fausto-Sterling, Anne. 2000. "The Five Sexes Revisited." *Sciences* 40, no. 4 (July/August): 18–24.

————. 1993. "The Five Sexes: Why Male and Female Are Not Enough." *Sciences* 33, no. 2 (March/April): 20–26.

Feagin, Joe R. 2000. *Racist America: Roots, Current Realities, and Future Reparations.* New York: Routledge.

————. 1991. "The Continuing Significance of Race: Anti-Black Discrimination in Public Places." *American Sociological Review* 56 (February): 101–116.

Federal Bureau of Investigation. 2004. "Hate Crime Statistics Press Release." http://fbi.gov/pressrel/pressrel02/01factsheethc.htm.

Fields, Reginald. 2004a. "City Fire Department Recruits 1st All-White Class in 50 Years." *Baltimore Sun,* April 20: 1A, 9A.

————. 2004b. "Fire Department Alters Hiring Policy." *Baltimore Sun,* April 23: 1B, 5B.

Files, John. 2005. "Ruling on Gays Exacts a Cost in Recruiting, a Study Finds." *New York Times,* February 24: A16.

Forbes. 2003. "Forbes Executive Pay." http://www.forbes.com/lists.

Forsythe, Jason. 2004. "Winning with Diversity." *New York Times Magazine,* September 19: 95–132.

————. 2003. "Diversity Works." *New York Times Magazine,* September 14: 75–100.

Frankel, Barbara, and Yoji Cole. 2004. "DiversityInc's Top 50 Companies for Diversity." http://www.diversityinc.com/members/6719print.cfm.

Freeman, Jo, and Victoria Johnson, eds. 1999. *Waves of Protest: Social Movements Since the Sixties.* Lanham, Md.: Rowman and Littlefield.

Frye, Marilyn. 1983. *The Politics of Reality: Essays in Feminist Theory.* Freedom, Calif.: Crossing.

GayDemographics.org. N.d. "PUMS Information, Same-Sex Couples." http://www.gaydemographics.org/USA/PUMS/nationalintro.htm.

Gay, Lesbian, and Straight Education Network. 2004. "The 2003 National School Climate Survey." http://www.glsen.org.

Gerstenfeld, Phyllis B. 2004. *Hate Crimes: Causes, Controls, and Controversies.* Thousand Oaks, Calif.: Sage.

Gibson, Gail. 2004. "Women Workers in US Have Bias in Common." *Baltimore Sun,* July 16: 1A, 11A.

Gilbert, Dennis. 1998. *The American Class Structure: In an Age of Growing Inequality.* 5th ed. Belmont, Calif.: Wadsworth.

Glenn, David. 2003. "The *Economist* as Affable Provocateur." *Chronicle of Higher Education,* December 5: A10–11.

Glick, P., and S. T. Fiske. 2001. "An Ambivalent Alliance: Hostile and Benevolent Sexism as Contemporary Justifications for Gender Inequality." *American Psychologist* 56, no. 2: 109–118.

————. 1996. "The Ambivalent Sexism Inventory: Differentiating Hostile and Benevolent Sexism." *Journal of Personality and Social Psychology* 70: 491–512.

Goldstein, Richard. 2003. "What the Sodomy Ruling Has Changed—and What It Hasn't." *Village Voice* online, July 2–8. http://www.villagevoice.com/issues/0327/goldstein.php.

Green Party. 2004. "Green Party Election Results." http://www.gp.org/2004election/pr_11_04.html.

Haniffa, Aziz. 2004. "Asian Groups Dispute FBI Report on Hate Crimes." *India Abroad,* December 10. Posted on http://www.portside.org.

Harrison, Lawrence E. 1992. *Who Prospers? How Cultural Values Shape Economic and Political Success.* New York: Basic.

Harvey, William B., and Eugene L. Anderson. 2005. *Minorities in Higher Education: Twenty-First Annual Status Report, 2003–2004.* Washington, D.C.: American Council on Education.

Healy, Patrick D., and Sara Rimer. 2005. "Furor Lingers as Harvard Chief Gives Details of Talk on Women." *New York Times,* February 18: A1, A16.

Hecker, Daniel E. 2004. "Occupational Employment Projections to 2012." *Monthly Labor Review,* February: 80–105.

Helwig, Ryan. 2004. "Worker Displacement in 1999–2000." *Monthly Labor Review,* June: 54–68.

Heyl, Barbara Sherman. 2003. "Homosexuality: A Social Phenomenon." In Karen E. Rosenblum and Toni-Michelle C. Travis (eds.), *The Meaning of Difference: American Constructions of Race, Sex, and Gender, Social Class, and Sexual Orientation.* 3rd ed. Boston: McGraw Hill.

Hiaasen, Rob. 2004. "One House, Many Voices." *Baltimore Sun,* December 11: 1D, 8D.

Hinrichs, Donald W., and Pamela J. Rosenberg. 2002. "Attitudes Toward Gay, Lesbian, and Bisexual Persons Among Heterosexual Liberal Arts College Students." *Journal of Homosexuality* 43, no. 1: 61–84.

Hirsch, Arthur, and Molly Knight. 2005. "Assaults Underreported at the Military Academies." *Baltimore Sun,* March 19: 1A, 4A.

Hofmann, Sudie. 2005. "Framing the Family Tree: How Teachers Can Be Sensitive to Students' Family Situations." *Rethinking Schools* 19 (Spring): 20–22.

hooks, bell. 2000. "Feminism: A Movement to End Sexist Oppression." In Maurianne Adams, et al. (eds.), *Readings for Diversity and Social Justice: An Anthology on Racism, Antisemitism, Sexism, Heterosexism, Ableism, and Classism.* New York: Routledge.

Hossfeld, Karen J. 1999. "Hiring Immigrant Women: Silicon Valley's 'Simple Formula.'" In Fred L. Pincus and Howard J. Ehrlich (eds.), *Race and Eth-*

nic Conflict: Contending Views on Prejudice, Discrimination, and Eth-noviolence. Boulder: Westview.

Human Rights Campaign. 2004a. "Answers to Questions About Marriage Equality." http://www.hrc.org.

————. 2004b. "Equality in the States: Gay, Lesbian, Bisexual, Transgender Americans and State Laws and Legislation in 2004." http://www.hrc.org.

Humphreys, Debra. 2000. "National Survey Finds Diversity Requirements Common Around the Country." *Diversity Digest.* http://www.diversityweb.org/Digest/F00/survey.html.

Hurst, Charles E. 2004. *Social Inequality: Forms, Causes, and Consequences.* 5th ed. Boston: Allyn and Bacon.

Infoplease. 2004. http://www.infoplease.com/ipa/A076218.html.

Institute for Policy Studies. 2005. "The Iraq Quagmire: The Mounting Costs of the Iraq War." www.ips-dc.org/iraq/quagmire/cow.pdf.

Johnson, Allen. 2001. *Privilege, Power, and Difference.* Mountain View, Calif.: Mayfield.

Johnson, Angela D. 2004a. "40% of Fortune 500 Now Offer Domestic-Partner Benefits." DiversityInc. http://www.diversityinc.com/members/6817print.cfm.

————. 2004b. "No Gay Honeymooners Welcome at This Resort." *DiversityInc,* March 9. www.diversityinc.com/members/6495print.cfm.

Jones, James M. 1997. *Prejudice and Racism.* 2nd ed. Hightstown, N.J.: McGraw-Hill.

Kahn, Robert. 2004. "Scholarships Reach Out to Gays in College." *Baltimore Sun,* October 5: 1C, 5C.

Katz, Jonathan Ned. 1995. *The Invention of Heterosexuality.* New York: Dutton/Penguin.

Kaufman, Cynthia. 2003. *Ideas for Action: Relevant Theory of Radical Change.* Cambridge, Mass.: South End.

Kelly, Christine, and Joel Lefkowitz. 2003. "Radical and Pragmatic: United Students Against Sweatshops." In John C. Berg (ed.), *Teamsters and Turtles? US Progressive Political Movements in the 21st Century.* Lanham, Md.: Rowman and Littlefield.

Kendall, Diana, ed. 1997. *Race, Class, and Gender in a Diverse Society: A Text-Reader.* Boston: Allyn and Bacon.

Kerbo, Harold R. 2003. *Social Stratification and Inequality: Class Conflict in Historical, Comparative, and Global Perspective.* 5th ed. Boston: McGraw Hill.

Kimmel, Michael S. 2004. "Inequality and Difference." In Lisa Heldke and Peg O'Connor (eds.), *Oppression, Privilege, and Resistance: Theoretical Perspectives on Racism, Sexism, and Heterosexism.* Boston: McGraw Hill.

King, J. L. 2004. *Living on the Down Low: A Journey into the Lives of "Straight" Black Men Who Sleep with Men.* New York: Broadway.

Kinsey, Alfred C., Wardell B. Pomeroy, Clyde E. Martin, and Paul H Gebhard. 1953. *Sexual Behavior in the Human Female.* Philadelphia: W. B. Saunders.

————. 1948. *Sexual Behavior in the Human Male.* Philadelphia: W. B. Saunders.

Kochhar, Rakesh. 2004. *The Wealth of Hispanic Households: 1996 to 2002.* Washington, D.C.: Pew Hispanic Center.

Ladd, Everett Carll, and Karlyn H. Bowman. 1998. *Attitudes Toward Economic Inequality.* Washington, D.C.: American Enterprise Institute for Public Policy Research.

Langfitt, Frank. 2004. "Violence, Bias Against Muslims up Nearly 70%." *Baltimore Sun,* May 4: 9A.

LeDuff, Charlie. 2000. "At a Slaughterhouse, Some Things Never Die." *New York Times,* June 16. http://www.nytimes.com.

Lewis, Gregory B. 2003. "Black-White Differences in Attitudes Toward Homosexuality and Gay Rights." *Public Opinion Quarterly* 67: 59–78.

Lorber, Judith. 1998. *Gender Equality: Feminist Theory and Politics.* Los Angeles: Roxbury.

Masser, Barbara, and Dominic Abrams. 1999. "Contemporary Sexism: The Relationships Among Hostility, Benevolence, and Neosexism." *Psychology of Women Quarterly* 23: 503–517.

McGeehan, Patrick. 2004a. "Discrimination on Wall St.? Run the Numbers and Weep." *New York Times,* July 14: C1, C7.

————. 2004b. "Morgan Stanley Settles Bias Suit with $54 Million." *New York Times,* July 13: A1, C9.

Meyer, David S. 2003. "How Social Movements Matter." *Contexts* 2, no. 4 (Fall): 30–35.

Mishel, Lawrence, Jared Bernstein, and Sylvia Allegretto. 2005. *The State of Working America: 2004–2005.* New York: Cornell University Press.

Morin, Monte, and Jessica Garrison. 2004. "City Settles Decade-Old Suits over Gender Bias." *Los Angeles Times,* December 16: B3.

Morrison, Melanie, and Todd G. Morrison. 2002. "Development and Validation of a Scale Measuring Modern Prejudice Toward Gay Men and Lesbian Women." *Journal of Homosexuality* 43, no. 2: 15–37.

Moser, Bob. 2005. "The Religious Crusade Against Gays Has Been Building for 30 Years. Now the Movement Is Reaching Truly Biblical Proportions." *Intelligence Report* 117 (Spring): 9–21.

Ness, Immanuel. 2003. "Unions and American Workers: Whither the Labor Movement?" In John C. Berg (ed.), *Teamsters and Turtles? US Progressive Political Movements in the 21st Century.* Lanham, Md.: Rowman and Littlefield.

New York Times/CBS News. 2005. "Class Project" poll. http://www.nytimes.com.

New York Times News Service. 2005. "United Church of Christ Endorses Gay Marriage. *Baltimore Sun,* July 5: 3A.

————. 2004. "Target Corp. Contractor Settles Labor Law Violations." *Baltimore Sun,* August 26: 1D, 10D.

O'Brien, Eileen. 2001. *Whites Confront Racism: Anti Racists and Their Paths to Activism.* New York: Rowman and Littlefield.

Ollenberger, Jane C., and Helen A. Moore. 1998. *A Sociology of Women: The Intersection of Patriarchy, Capitalism, and Colonization.* 2nd ed. Upper Saddle River, N.J.: Prentice Hall.

Ore, Tracy E., ed. 2003. *The Social Construction of Difference and Inequality.* 2nd ed. Boston: McGraw Hill.

Orfield, Gary. 2001. *Diversity Challenged: Evidence on the Impact of Affirmative Action.* Cambridge, Mass.: Civil Rights Project, Harvard Publishing Group.

Ortiz, Peter. 2004a. "Another Huge Gender-Bias Settlement: Boeing to Pay up to $72.5 Million." *DiversityInc,* July 17. http://www.diversityinc.com/members/7678print.cfm.

———. 2004b. "Women of Color Are on a Buying Spree." *DiversityInc.* http://www.diversityinc.com/members/7495print.cfm.

Pager, Devah. 2003. "The Mark of a Criminal Record." *American Journal of Sociology* 108 (March): 937–975.

Pincus, Fred L. 2003. *Reverse Discrimination: Dismantling the Myth.* Boulder, Colo.: Lynne Rienner.

Pincus, Fred L., and Howard J. Ehrlich, eds. 1999. *Race and Ethnic Conflict: Contending Views on Prejudice, Discrimination, and Ethnoviolence.* Boulder, Colo.: Westview.

Pinkus, Susan, and Jill Darling Richardson. 2004. "Americans Oppose Same-Sex Marriage but Acceptance of Gays in Society Grows." *Los Angeles Times* Poll/Gay Issues Survey, Study #501. http://www.latimes.com.

Price, Barbara Raffel, and Natalie J. Sokoloff, eds. 2004. *The Criminal Justice System and Women: Offenders, Prisoners, Victims, and Workers.* 3rd ed. Boston: McGraw Hill.

Rai, Saritha. 2004. "An Outsourcing Giant Fights Back." *New York Times,* March 21: 3:A1, 10.

Renzetti, Claire M., and Daniel J. Curran. 1999. *Women, Men, and Society.* 4th ed. Boston: Allyn and Bacon.

Rosenblum, Karen E., and Toni-Michelle C. Travis, eds. 2003. *The Meaning of Difference: American Constructions of Race, Sex, and Gender, Social Class, and Sexual Orientation.* 3rd ed. Boston: McGraw Hill.

Roth, Byron. 1994. "Racism and Traditional American Values." *Studies in Social Philosophy and Policy* 18: 119–140.

Rothenberg, Paula S., ed. 2004. *Race, Class, and Gender in the United States.* 6th ed. New York: Worth.

Sachdev, Ameet. 2004. "Accountants Next Target for Underdog and Underdog." *Baltimore Sun,* May 3. http://www.baltimoresun.com.

Salz, Arthur, and Julius Trubowitz. 1999. "It Was All of Us Working Together: Resolving Racial and Ethnic Tension on College Campuses." In Fred L. Pincus and Howard J. Ehrlich (eds.), *Race and Ethnic Conflict: Contending Views on Prejudice, Discrimination, and Ethnoviolence.* Boulder, Colo.: Westview.

Savin-Williams, Ritch C., and Kenneth M. Cohen. 1996. *The Lives of Lesbians, Gays, and Bisexuals: Children to Adults.* Fort Worth: Harcourt Brace.

Scarborough, Rowan. 2004. "Report Leans Toward Women in Combat." *Washington Times,* December 1. www.washtimes.com.

Seid, Judith. 2001. *Good Optional Judaism.* New York: Citadel Press.

Shepard, Benjamin. 2003. "The AIDS Coalition to Unleash Power: A Brief Reconsideration." In John C. Berg (ed.), *Teamsters and Turtles? US Progressive Political Movements in the 21st Century.* Lanham, Md.: Rowman and Littlefield.

Shin, Annys. 2005. "$80 Million Settles Race-Bias Case." *Washington Post,* April 28: A1.

Smith, David M., and Gary J. Gates. 2001. "Gay and Lesbian Families in the United States: Same-Sex Unmarried Partner Households." Human Rights Campaign. http://www.hrc.org.

Southern Poverty Law Center. 2004. "Center Responds to Hate and Bias on Campuses." *SPLC Report* 34 (March): 1, 5.

Spence, J. T., and E. D. Hahn. 1997. "The Attitudes Toward Women Scale and Attitude Change in College Students." *Psychology of Women Quarterly* 21: 17–34.

Spence, J. T., R. Helmreich, and J. Stapp. 1973. "A Short Version of the Attitudes Toward Women Scale (AWS)." *Psychology of Women Quarterly* 2: 219–220.

Spiro, Leah Nathans. 1996. "Smith Barney's Woman Problem." *Business Week,* June 3. http://www.businessweek.com/1996.

Stepp, Laura Sessions. 2003. "In La. School, Son of Lesbian Learns 'Gay' Is a 'Bad Wurd.'" *Washington Post,* December 3: C1, C10.

Swarns, Rachel L. 2004. "Hispanics Debate Racial Grouping by Census." *New York Times*, October 24: A1, A18.

Swim, Janet K., Kathryn J. Aikin, Wayne S. Hall, and Barbara A. Hunter. 1995. "Sexism and Racism: Old-Fashioned and Modern Prejudices." *Journal of Personality and Social Psychology* 68, no. 2: 199–214.

Swim, Janet K., and Bernadette Campbell. 2001. "Sexism: Attitudes, Beliefs, and Behaviors." *Blackwell Handbook of Social Psychology: Intergroup Processes.* Malden, Mass.: Blackwell.

Swim, Janet K., and Laurie L. Cohen. 1997. "Overt, Covert, and Subtle Sexism." *Psychology of Women Quarterly* 21: 103–118.

Takaki, Ronald. 1993. *A Different Mirror: A History of Multicultural America.* Boston: Back Bay Books.

Tatum, Beverly Daniel. 2003. *"Why Are All the Black Kids Sitting Together in the Cafeteria? And Other Conversations About Race.* New York: Basic.

Thomas, Cal. 2004. "A Rear-Guard Effort to Put Women in Combat." *Baltimore Sun,* December 22: 23A.

Tougas, F., R. Brown, A. M. Beaton, and S. Joly. 1995. "Neosexism: *Plus ca change, plus c'est pareil." Psychology of Women Quarterly* 21: 842–849.

Turner, Jonathan H., Royce Singleton Jr., and David Musick. 1984. *Oppression: A Socio-History of Black-White Relations in America.* Chicago: Nelson Hall.

United for a Fair Economy. 1999. "CEO Paycharts." http://www.ufenet.org/ research/CEO_Pay_charts.html.

———. 1997. "Born on Third Base: The Sources of Wealth of the 1997 Forbes 400." http://www.faireconomy.org/press/archive/Pre_1999/forbes_400_ study_1997.html.

US Bureau of Labor Statistics. 2004. Table 11. "Employed Persons by Detailed Occupation, Sex, Race, and Hispanic or Latino Ethnicity." www.bls.gov.

US Census Bureau. 2004. "Census Bureau Projects Tripling of Hispanic and Asian Populations in 50 Years; Non-Hispanic Whites May Drop to Half of Total Population." Press release, March 18. Washington, D.C.: US Department of Commerce. http://www.census.gov/popest/national/asrh/ NC-EST2003-srj.html.

———. 2004a. *Statistical Abstract of the United States.* www.census.gov/ statab/www/.

———. 2003a. *Income in the United States: 2002.* Washington, D.C.: US Department of Commerce. http://www.census.gov.

———. 2003b. *Net Worth and Asset Ownership of Households: 1998 and 2000.* Washington, D.C.: US Department of Commerce. http://www. census.gov.

———. 2003c. *Poverty in the United States: 2002.* Washington, D.C.: US Department of Commerce. http://www.census.gov.

———. 1995. *Household Wealth and Asset Ownership: 1993.* Washington, D.C.: US Department of Commerce. http://www.census.gov/prod/1/pop/ p70-47.pdf.

US General Accounting Office. 2003. "Women's Earnings: Work Patterns Partially Explain Difference Between Men's and Women's Earnings." GAO-04-35, October. Washington, D.C.: General Accounting Office.

Vandenburgh, Reid. 2005. Personal communication.

Walker, Andrea K. 2004. "Giants of Retail." *Baltimore Sun*, March 21: 1D, 2D.

Watanabe, Teresa, and Nancy Wride. 2004. "Stark Contrasts Found Among Asian Americans." *Los Angeles Times,* December 16: A1, A33.

Weeden, Kim A. 2004. "Profiles of Change: Sex Segregation in the United States, 1910–2000." In Maria Charles and David B. Grusky (eds.), *Occupational Ghettos: The Worldwide Segregation of Women and Men.* Stanford, Calif.: Stanford University Press.

Weinberg, Daniel. 2004. "Evidence from Census 2000 About Earnings by Detailed Occupation for Men and Women." CENSR-15, May. http://www. census.gov/newonsite.

Weinberg, Rick. 2002. "Smith Barney Wins Arbitration Order in 'Boom Boom' Case." *Registered Rep.* http://registeredrep.com.

Weinraub, Bernard, and Jim Rutenberg. 2003. "Gay-Themed TV Gains a Wider Audience." *New York Times* online, July 29. http://www.nytimes.com.

Welch, Ed. 2004. "TV's Disappearing Gays." http://www.365gay.com.

Werschkul, Misha, and Jody Herman. 2004. "New IWPR Report Addresses Women's Employment Equity and Earnings: How Many More Years Until

Equality?" *Institute for Women's Policy Research Quarterly Newsletter* (Winter/Spring): 1, 7.

Wilson, Robin. 2004. "Where the Elite Teach, It's Still a Man's World." *Chronicle of Higher Education* 51, no. 15 (December 3): 8–14.

Wire Services. 2005. "Wal-Mart Agrees to Pay $11 Million to Settle Illegal-Immigrant Case." *Baltimore Sun,* March 19: 13C–14C.

Wood, Peter. 2003. *Diversity: The Invention of a Concept.* San Francisco: Encounter.

Wright, Erik Olin. 1997. *Class Counts: Student Edition.* New York: Cambridge University Press.

Yates, Michael D. 2005. "A Statistical Portrait of the US Working Class." *Monthly Review* 56 (April): 12–31.

Zack, Naomi, Laurie Shrage, and Crispin Sartwell. 1998. *Race, Class, Gender, and Sexuality: The Big Questions.* Malden, Mass.: Blackwell.

Zinn, Howard. 2003. *A People's History of the United States: 1492–Present.* New York: Perennial Classics.

Zurawik, David. 2005. "Despite Denunciation, 'Buster' Episode to Air." *Baltimore Sun,* February 1: 1A, 6A.

Zweig, Michael. 2000. *The Working Class Majority: America's Best Kept Secret.* Ithaca, N.Y.: Cornell University Press.

Index

electoral, 123–124; liberals in, 26–27; radicals in, 27
Postcards from Buster (television), 113, 114
Poverty, 37, 38; "blame the victim" approach, 43; causes of, 44; culture of, 44; explanations for, 42, 43; government action and, 44
Power: decision-making, 31; hierarchy of inequality in, 4; patriarchal, 79, 80; political, 6; racism and, 57
Prejudice: class and, 41–44; conservatism and, 70; decline of, 69; defining, 19; dominant group, 19; ethnic views on, 69; gender and, 90–92; homosexuality and, 107–111; multidirectional, 19; negative attitudes in, 70–71; "new," 70, 91; race and, 19, 69–71; religion and, 111; sexual orientation and, 107–111; traditional, 69, 70, 110
President's Commission on the Status of Women, 130
Price, Barbara, 5, 81
Privilege: defining, 15; denial of, 16; hierarchy of inequality in, 4; recognition of, 16
Pseudohermaphroditism, 78
Purdue, Frank, 41

Race, 51–76; class/gender issues and, 4, 5; cultural concept of, 52; defining, 51–59; descriptive statistics in, 59–68; discrimination and, 71–76; distribution of same-sex partners, 103; employment discrimination and, 72, 73; employment/unemployment rates and, 59, 59*tab*, 60, 60*tab*, 61, 61*tab*; essentialism and, 12; ethnicity and, 53–55; feminism and, 5; genetic variations in, 52; hate crimes and, 72; ideology and, 69–71; income and, 61, 61*tab*, 62,

63, 63*tab*, 64, 64*tab*; majority/minority group status and, 11; one-drop rule and, 52, 53; pejorative terminology and, 58; poverty and, 63, 64; prejudice and, 19, 69–71; relations, 4; riots and, 6, 129; sexual orientation and, 112, 113; social construction of, 52; social movements and, 125–130; sociocultural determinations in, 12
Racial: attitudes toward homosexuality, 109; conflict, 51; differences, 4; distribution of population, 54, 54*tab*, 55; passing, 52; profiling, 75; separation, 69; stereotypes, 18; stigmatization, 52
Racism: aversive, 70; color-blind, 70, 71; defining, 56–59; dominant group and, 57; labels in, 57, 58, 59; laissez-faire, 70; modern, 70; oppression and, 57; power and, 57; symbolic, 70; systemic, 56–57
Radicalism, 27; educational policy and, 123; social movements and, 122
Rainbow Coalition, 123
Randolph, A. Phillip, 127
Religion, 1; Christian fundamentalism, 25; Christianity, 56; ethnicity and, 55, 56; gay issues and, 108–109; homosexuality and, 111; institutional discrimination by, 95, 115; Islam, 56; prejudice and, 111
Rights: civil, 25, 26, 69, 71, 112, 116, 124, 128–131; gay, 25, 26, 108; immigrant, 135; women's, 26, 125; worker's, 127, 132–134
Riots, 6, 129
Robber barons, 126
Robeson, Paul, 127
Rockefeller, David, 41
Rockefeller, John D., 126
Role: defining, 10; status and, 10
Roosevelt, Franklin, 127

University of Worcester

ILS at the University of Worcester

Peirson Building
University of Worcester
Henwick Grove
Worcester
WR2 6AJ

Items Borrowed

Borrower : MISS ELIZABETH M

- Understanding diversity : an introduction to class, race, gender, and sexual (Barcode: A1057957)
  Due Date : 29/03/2011 17:00

Issue date: 22/03/2011 10:31 1 1319

Remember you can renew your books using Library Resources Online

or Tel: 01905 855341

Thank you for using the ILS Department

Please keep this receipt as proof of this transaction

About the Book

What is diversity? How does prejudice show itself? What are the societal consequences of discrimination—toward women, toward gays, toward people of color, toward the poor? Has anything changed over the past forty years? These are just some of the questions addressed in this introduction to the issues and controversies surrounding the concepts of race, class, gender, and sexual orientation.

The opening chapter of *Understanding Diversity* establishes both the importance of the subject—in a real-life way—and the necessity of a multilevel approach to exploring it. Chapters on race, gender, class, and sexual orientation are then organized around six consistent themes: terminology, descriptive statistics, concepts of prejudice, social construction, discrimination, and social movements. A discussion of the politics of diversity compellingly demonstrates the role of theory in the search for strategies to combat oppression.

Accessible and practical, yet theoretically rich, *Understanding Diversity* is the perfect companion to the many diversity anthologies on the market.

Fred L. Pincus is professor of sociology at the University of Maryland–Baltimore County. He is author of *Reverse Discrimination: Dismantling the Myth* and coeditor of *Race and Ethnic Conflict: Contending Views on Prejudice, Discrimination, and Ethnoviolence*.